UNIVERSITY OF NORTH CAROLINA
STUDIES IN THE ROMANCE LANGUAGES AND LITERATURES
Number 37

THE REAPPEARING CHARACTERS
IN
BALZAC'S *COMÉDIE HUMAINE*

THE REAPPEARING CHARACTERS
IN
BALZAC'S *COMÉDIE HUMAINE*

BY

ARTHUR GRAVES CANFIELD

EDITED BY

EDWARD B. HAM

CHAPEL HILL

THE UNIVERSITY OF NORTH CAROLINA PRESS

Depósito Legal: V. 2.681 – 1961

TABLE OF CONTENTS

	Page
PREFACE (A. G. C.)	VII
EDITOR'S NOTE	IX

Chapter

		Page
I.	GENESIS OF BALZAC'S PLAN FOR REAPPEARING CHARACTERS	1
II.	THE GROWTH OF THE WORLD OF REAPPEARING CHARACTERS	7
III.	GROUPING OF REAPPEARERS IN INDIVIDUAL STORIES	13
IV.	CHANGES DUE TO INTERPOLATION OR SUBSTITUTION OF NAMES	19
V.	CHRONOLOGICAL INCONSISTENCIES IN THE "COMÉDIE HUMAINE"	25
VI.	FURTHER INCONSISTENCIES AND CONTRADICTIONS	35
VII.	NUMBER AND IMPORTANCE OF INDIVIDUAL REAPPEARERS	43
APPENDIX A		47
APPENDIX B		51

PREFACE

The purpose of this study is to fix the point of origin of Balzac's technique of reappearing characters and to trace its development. It seeks to give a history of the beginning and gradual expansion of the various groups of reappearing characters. Unfortunately, *all* the materials could not be reached, and the comparison of the editions which I have been unable to consult may here and there add a detail to supplement the information here presented. It cannot, I am convinced, appreciably affect the account here given of the formation of the world of the *Comédie humaine* which it was Balzac's ambition to make a complete counterpart of the society of his time.

This study also aims to assemble information needed for an evaluation of this technique and an appreciation of its contribution to the total effect for which Balzac strove in creating his imaginary world. Incidentally, it points out certain inconsistencies and contradictions between different stories which sometimes resulted. It suggests also the light that the study of reappearing characters may throw on the history, still to be written, of the composition of the *Comédie humaine* to supplement the indispensable history of its publication that we now have in the *Histoire des oeuvres de H. de Balzac* by the vicomte de Lovenjoul and in *Balzac romancier* by Maurice Bardèche.

A. G. C.

Ann Arbor (Michigan), 1947.

EDITOR'S NOTE

Professor Arthur Graves Canfield died in Ann Arbor, December fifth, 1947, shortly before his eighty-ninth birthday. For nearly two decades after his retirement as Chairman of the Department of Romance Languages at the University of Michigan, he had been preparing the data and text for the Balzac research presented here. Mrs. Canfield, who survived her husband until 1954, graciously made all of his Balzac papers available, thereby making publication of this monograph possible.

Professor Canfield's manuscript was complete except for its final chapter and except for review of previous studies (including his own) on Balzac's reappearing characters. Accordingly, this introductory note is intended only as a brief supplement to the monograph proper. Primarily, however, the reader should welcome the fact that Professor Canfield's discussion now appears, virtually entire, in his own phraseology: minor oversights have needed only minimal editing; also, the two appendices which I have added are self-explanatory.

It is with pleasure and gratitude that I acknowledge the generous support for publication of the present monograph: from this series at the University of North Carolina, and from funds derived from income on the endowment of the Horace H. Rackham School of Graduate Studies at the University of Michigan.

While it is not possible to intimate the contents of the final chapter which Professor Canfield did not live to write, it is equally superfluous to annotate a monograph which is already its author's clear and closely knit entity. It is, however, evident that his manuscript would have included a critical survey of earlier work on reappearing characters in the *Comédie humaine*. To date, the more important investigations by other scholars (with the abbreviations used *infra*) are:

Preston. — Ethel Preston, *Recherches sur la technique de Balzac: le Retour systématique des personnages dans la "Comédie humaine"* (Paris, 1926).

Bardèche. — Maurice Bardèche, *Balzac romancier* (Paris, 1940): cf. in particular, pp. 518 ff. A somewhat condensed revision of this thesis was published, with the same title, in 1943.

Dargan-Weinberg. — *The Evolution of Balzac's "Comédie humaine"*, edited by E. Preston Dargan and Bernard Weinberg (Chicago, 1942).

Lotte. — Fernand Lotte, *Dictionnaire biographique des personnages fictifs de la "Comédie humaine"* (Paris, 1952). A 91-page supplement was published in 1956, to acount for the anonymous characters (for reappearers, cf. pp. 70-79).

Félicien Marceau, *Balzac et son monde* (Paris, 1955): a pleasantly semi-popularized catalogue, with value for acquaintance with the reappearing characters.

Of the collective editions of Balzac, only the following have been utilized by Professor Canfield (others, such as the Pléiade text, are not essential for the study of reappearing characters):

Furne. — *La Comédie Humaine*, vols. I-XVIII (Paris, 1842-1855).

EdDéf. — *Oeuvres complètes*, ed. Calmann-Lévy (24 vols., Paris, 1869-1876). This edition, based on *Furne* and on Balzac's notations in his personal copy of *Furne*, is traditionally regarded as the "édition définitive" of his novels and stories.

Conard. — *Oeuvres complètes*, ed. Marcel Bouteron and Henri Longnon (40 vols., Paris, 1912-1940).

Allem refers to variorum editions of a number of the stories, as prepared during the past three decades by Maurice Allem(and). Abbreviations for pre-*Furne* texts mentioned here are accounted for in individual chapters, as the need arises.

Professor Canfield published three articles which serve as excellent preliminaries to his present monograph:

1) "Balzac's Technique of reappearing characters", *Papers of the Michigan Academy of Science, Arts and Letters,* XII (1929: published 1930), 267-273.

2) "Notes on Lovenjoul's *Histoire des Oeuvres de H. de Balzac*", *Modern Language Notes,* XLVIII (1933), 497-501.

3) "Les Personnages reparaissants dans 'La Comédie humaine' ", *Revue d'Histoire Littéraire,* XLI (1934), 15-31, 198-214.

In the first of these papers, Professor Canfield easily refuted the long-standing supposition that "the idea of reappearing characters was first applied in *Père Goriot*". Nonetheless this supposition persisted in a 'pot-boiler' essay written as recently as 1948 (*Atlantic Monthly,* CLXXXI, 51) where, however, W. Somerset Maugham somewhat redeemed himself by saying that with the reappearing characters Balzac's "aim was not to depict a group, a set, a class, or even a society, but a period and a civilization... He had the self-assurance to create a world, multicolored, various, and profuse, and the power to give it the convincing throb of life".

This note, finally, would not be complete without mention of the chapter which Professor Canfield began within only a few days of his death. While it would be presumptuous to suggest the plan which he had in mind, it is of evident interest here to reproduce the only existing part; especially as this first paragraph, composed after his operation in late November, was the last page that Professor Canfield ever wrote:

"Just as there were two ways of increasing the groups of reappearing characters, a natural and an artificial one, so their reappearance itself may be natural or artificial, arbitrary and contrived. In the three parts of *Illusions perdues* (*Les Deux Poètes, Un Grand Homme de province à Paris,* and *Eve et David*) and in two of *Splendeurs et Misères des courtisanes* and *La Dernière Incarnation de Vautrin,* which together form really one long story, there must be a group of actors common to some if not to all of the parts. So *Les Petits Bourgeois* returns to the scene of *Les Employés,* and there is a large group of characters common to the two. In *La Vieille Fille* and *Le Cabinet des Antiques,* the scene is laid in the small provincial city of Alençon and it is natural that certain characters appear in both..."

CHAPTER I

GENESIS OF BALZAC'S PLAN FOR REAPPEARING CHARACTERS

From the first Balzac thought of his works as parts of a whole rather than as independent and self-sufficient units. More than once he defended himself against his critics by telling them that they must wait till they had seen some other parts not yet built before judging of the edifice he was constructing. So it was natural that he should seek some means of giving an outward and visible bond of unity to these scenes that in his intention were related parts of one play, the "Human Comedy". We can well understand the excitement and elation he felt when he thought he had discoveret it. "The day when this idea dawned upon him was a great day for him", his sister writes, and she recalls the boyish enthusiasm and exultation with which he burst in upon her, having rushed straightway from his quarters in the rue Cassini to announce his triumph. "Salute me", he cried, "for I am fairly on the road to being a genius".[1] Speaking through the mouth of Félix Davin, who wrote for him the *Introduction aux Etudes de moeurs au XIX⁰ siècle* in 1835, Balzac insists upon the importance of his new idea: "A great step forward has recently been taken", he writes, "when the reader saw reappear in *Le Père Goriot* some of the characters already created, he came to understand one of the author's boldest intentions, that of giving life and movement to a whole fictitious world whose characters will perhaps live on when the greater part of their originals will be dead and forgotten".[2]

---

[1] *EdDéf*, XXIV (1876), 28.
[2] Cf. Lovenjoul, p. 56.

Madame Surville places her brother's announcement of his "discovery" in the year 1833. But there is no trace of it in the works that came from that year and the following, before *Le Père Goriot*. We must believe that he would not fail to exploit his idea at the first opportunity. Yet in *Eugénie Grandet*, *La Recherche de l'absolu*, *L'Illustre Gaudissart*, *Souffrances inconnues* and *La Vallée du torrent*, there was no character that appeared in any other story. Even in *Ferragus* and *La Duchesse de Langeais*, which were two parts of one story—the *Histoire des Treize*—and in which we might have expected to find at least thirteen characters in common, there are but four of the "Treize" who appear in both. It is not until *Le Père Goriot*, published at the very end of 1834 and during the first days of 1835, that we encounter the "reappearing characters" that were the realization of his grand idea.

It is true that Pauline Salomon de Villenoix appears both in *Louis Lambert* and *Le Curé de Tours*, in 1832. But aside from the name, there is little to identify the two as one and the same person. Mademoiselle de Villenoix of *Le Curé de Tours* had indeed for five years devoted herself to the care of her demented fiancé. But the Pauline of *Louis Lambert* was in 1820 in the full flush of youth; Mademoiselle de Villenoix is described in *Le Curé de Tours* as belonging to the *città dolente* of "vieilles filles". In *Louis Lambert* "the origin of Mademoiselle de Villenoix and the prejudices that persist in the provinces against the Jews did not permit her, in spite of her fortune, to be received in that society which calls itself, rightly or wrongly, the Nobility". In *Le Curé de Tours* she moves in the same circle with Madame de Listomère and belongs to the "most aristocratic society in Tours". Evidently, the rôle of Madame de Villenoix is not that of the typical reappearing character; she does not recall a group of known persons or represent a definite social region.

Another name had reappeared in *La Duchesse de Langeais*. The duchess, ardently pursued by Montriveau, cites the warning example of Madame de Beauséant who, in *La Femme abandonnée*, had sacrificed her position for the love of the marquis d'Ajuda-Pinto. "La rupture qu'on prévoit", she says, "entre madame de Beauséant et monsieur d'Ajuda, qui, dit-on, épouse mademoiselle de Rochefide, m'a prouvé que ces mêmes sacrifices sont presque toujours les causes de votre abandon". And again later, she declares that she will not "faire une seconde édition de madame de Beauséant".[3] But such a reference to the adventure of Madame de Beauséant does not oblige us to conclude that the device of reappearing characters had already occurred to Balzac. Balzac, who so readily confused the world of his imagination with the world of reality, did not need his system to invoke here this striking example of the fragility of human attachments.[4] In a third passage in *La Duchesse de Langeais* in which Madame de Beauséant's name now appears, it was not present in the first edition, but was substituted in a later edition for that of Madame de Sérisy.

Another example of the appearance of the same character in two stories occurs in the *Oeuvres de jeunesse*. Argow of *Le Vicaire des Ardennes* is the hero of *Argow le pirate*. But this does not imply a technique of reappearing characters any more than does the reappearance of Sherlock Holmes in one adventure after another. The same is true of the appearance of the marquis de Ronquerolles and his sister (Madame de Sérisy) in *Ferragus* and *La Duchesse de Langeais*, and of Henri de Marsay in *La Duchesse de Langeais* and *La Fille aux yeux d'or*. These three stories were parts of the *Histoire des Treize*. After reading the preface, one is surprised that there are not at least thirteen characters common to all three (cf. *supra*). Of the famous Thirteen who "recommencèrent la société de Jésus au profit du diable", only four are named: Henri de Marsay, the marquis de Ronquerolles, the marquis de Montriveau, and Ferragus (Auguste de Maulincour just possibly qualifies as a fifth). Of the four, only Marsay and Ronquerolles figured originally in more than one story. Ronquerolles alone appeared in all three. If the idea of making his characters reappear had occurred to Balzac before he

---

[3] In both these passages the text of the first edition (Béchet, *Scènes de la vie parisienne*, III 1834) is somewhat different. The first reads (p. 126; cf. *Conard*, 223): "La récente aventure de madame de Beauséant m'a prouvé" etc.; the second (p. 158; cf. *Conard*, 243) "...faire une seconde édition de l'histoire de madame de Beauséant".

[4] One can hardly avoid the conjecture that there may be here in *La Duchesse de Langeais* an echo of conversations of Balzac and Madame de Castries at Aix in 1832, when he was so much in her company and trying to play the same rôle towards her that Montriveau plays towards Madame de Langeais. It was just at that time that *La Femme abandonnée*, the story of Madame de Beauséant's adventure, was published in the *Revue de Paris*, XLII (September 1832), 113-138, 172-190; Balzac and Madame de Castries must certainly have discussed it together.

had finished the *Histoire des Treize,* we must certainly think that he would have at once exploited his idea there, where there was every opportunity and even provocation to do so. The absence of reappearing characters also in *Eugénie Grandet* and *L'Illustre Gaudissart,* which were written in 1833, further supports the conclusion that the visit so vividly described by Madame Surville could not have been made so early as 1833.[5]

There is a bit of evidence that tends to show that Balzac's discovery was not made until after he had begun work on *Le Père Goriot.* In the first pages of the manuscript of that work, the name of the hero is not Rastignac.[6] This would seem to mean that when the character of his hero was conceived and first sketched, Balzac did not have in mind the Rastingnac of *La Peau de chagrin.* Indeed, Roques discovers certain inconsistencies between the two characters. Would this have been possible had Balzac already formed his plan of reappearing characters?

There were, however, before the appearance of *Le Père Goriot* certain indications that Balzac was in possession of his idea and was already beginning to exploit it. In the summer of 1834, while he was at work on *Le Père Goriot,* he was also revising the *Scènes de la vie privée* for a third edition. In September, the fourth volume of that edition was issued (by Madame Béchet), containing, under the title *Même Histoire,* the six stories forming the chapters of *La Femme de trente ans.* Though they were loosely united by the title, they were still entirely separate and independent, the central characters having different names in the various episodes. They are the marquis and marquise d'Aiglemont only in the first, *Le Rendez-vous.* In the third chapter they are the marquis and marquise de Vieumesnil. The

---

[5] Not too much reliance can be placed on the accuracy of Madame Surville's memory, as is abundantly shown in her biographical sketch of her illustrious brother. What seems to have fixed the year 1833 in her mind as the time of this visit is an association with *Le Médecin de campagne,* published by Mame-Delaunay in September of that year. But there was a second edition of *Le Médecin de campagne* published by Werdet in 1834, and it seems to have given Balzac quite as much trouble as the first.

[6] Cf. the interesting study by Mario Roques in *Revue Universitaire,* XIV[2] (1905), 34-42, 71-76, 178-183; partially reprinted in the author's *Etudes de littérature française de la Chanson de Roland à Guillaume Apollinaire* (Lille-Geneva, 1949), pp. 107-115. Cf. also Jean Pommier, *Revue d'Histoire Littéraire,* L (1950), 192-209.

name of Madame de Vieumesnil's hostess in the opening scene is not Madame Firmiani, but Madame Vitagliano. The callers whose visits the marchioness recalls during the absence of Charles de Vandenesse (*Conard* VI, 124) were not originally Ronquerolles and Marsay, but Blamont and Vouglans. In the third edition, Madame de Vieumesnil is still Madame de Vieumesnil, Madame Vitagliano still Madame Vitagliano. But Ronquerolles and Marsay have replaced Blamont and Vouglans.[7] Such a substitution of names would hardly have been made had not Balzac already conceived having his characters reappear.

Another hint that Balzac was at this time in possession of his idea is to be found in the same volume of this third edition of *Scènes de la vie privée*, in *La Vallée du torrent*. This second part of *Le Doigt de Dieu*, the fourth of the stories brought together under the title of *Même Histoire*, appeared here for the first time. In it Alexandre Crottat figures as the notary of the marquis (*Conard* VI, 142): it is true that Crottat had not previously appeared, but he plays a very important part in *César Birotteau*. Although this novel was not published till the end of 1837, we know that it had been begun long before. Balzac put much work on it early in 1834 and even announced that it was ready for publication.[8] As early as 1830 the figure of the *parfumeur* seems to have been haunting his imagination.[9] The reader of *César Birotteau* cannot doubt that the character, if not the name, belonged to that story from the beginning. It seems pro-

---

[7] The text of *Mame* (p. 202): "M. de Blamont et M. de Vouglans sont restés ici, l'un hier, l'autre ce matin, près de deux heures". In *Conard* (p. 124), this has become: "Monsieur de Ronquerolles et monsieur de Marsay, le petit d'Esgrignon, sont restés ici, l'un hier, l'autre ce matin, près de deux heures. J'ai vu, je crois, aussi, madame Firmiani et votre soeur, madame de Listomère". The only change from *Mame* to *Béchet* (p. 229) is the substitution of Ronquerolles and Marsay for Blamont and Vouglans. The names of Madame Firmiani and Madame de Listomère were added in *Werdet* (p. 91), and the name "Esgrignon" was added in *Furne* (p. 95). In introducing the latter, Balzac apparently did not notice that the following "l'un hier, l'autre ce matin" no longer quite fits.

[8] Cf. Maurice Serval, "Autour de Balzac — *César Birotteau*", *Revue d'Histoire Littéraire*, XXXVII (1930), 196-226, 368-392.

[9] Cf. Gilbert M. Fess, *Modern Language Notes*, XLIX (1934), 516 ff.

bable that in *La Vallée du torrent* Crottat was virtually a reappearing character.[10]

Everything points, then, to the summer of 1834, when Balzac was beginning *Le Père Goriot*, as the time when he was illumined by his brilliant idea.

---

[10] One may conjecture that it was only an afterthought to identify the notary of *La Vallée du torrent* with the one of *César Birotteau*: they have nothing in common but the name.

CHAPTER II

THE GROWTH OF THE WORLD OF REAPPEARING
CHARACTERS

Le Père Goriot was the first work written after Balzac was in possession of his idea; in it the results of his new technique are evident (cf. Bardèche, pp. 501 ff.). Of the characters figuring in Le Père Goriot at least thirty-five had been created in earlier stories (notably Histoire des Treize, La Femme abandonnée, Gobseck). Numerous of these reappearers are merely mentioned, have no part in the action and, if they come upon the stage at all, are only supernumeraries.[1] One is a servant (Jacques; Conard VI, pp. 293, 484); the vicomte de Beauséant hardly appears (p. 287); the rôle of the marquis de Montriveau is negligible (p. 255), and that of the duchesse de Carigliano hardly less so (pp. 255, 348, 353, 378). Only eight of the reappearing characters take any real part in the action: the marquis d'Ajuda-Pinto (pp. 255, 289-296, 349-350, 473, 484-485); the vicomtesse de Beauséant (pp. 253, 281, 287-308); Gobseck (pp. 262, 268, 452, 462, 477); the duchesse de Langeais (pp. 255, 294-301, 484-487); Henri de Marsay (pp. 255, 303, 349, 353, 358, 374, 466); the comte de Restaud and his wife (pp. 254 ff.); Eugène de Rastignac (passim). To these should be added Maxime de Trailles (pp. 255 ff.), for, though his name did not occur in the original version

---

[1] E. g., the marquise d'Aiglemont (Julie de Châtillonest), Lady Brandon, Madame Firmiani, the comtesse de Kergarouët, the comtesse de Sérisy, all mentioned in Conard VI, pp. 255-256; the marquis de Beauséant (p. 287); the duc de Carigliano (p. 340); Derville (pp. 376, 454); Auguste de Maulincourt, Charles de Vandenesse, and Ronquerolles (p. 255); Ernest de Restaud (p. 463.

of *Gobseck*, no reader of that story could fail to recognize his rôle in *Le Père Goriot* as the object of Madame de Restaud's infatuation.

In its present form, as it appears since the publication of *EdDéf*, *Le Père Goriot* has added four supernumeraries to the group standing in the background and merely dressing the stage (pp. 255-256): the marquise d'Espard from *L'Interdiction*, the comtesse Ferraud from *Le Colonel Chabert*, the comtesse de Lanty from *Sarrasine*, and Diane de Maufrigneuse from *Le Cabinet des Antiques*. The total number of reappearing characters, however, has grown to upwards of seventy. Also some two dozen characters "created" in *Le Père Goriot* became reappearers by returning to the stage in later stories.

There were thus two ways in wich Balzac increased the number of reappearing characters. The first was by bringing a character created in an earlier book again upon the scene in a new one; the second was by adding in a new edition of an old work a name which originally had been absent. The first we may call the natural and, as it were, organic way. The second appears artificial and arbitrary. We shall find both methods used throughout the process of creation of the world of the *Comédie Humaine*.

Let us first see how this world grew by the natural way, by the continual recall in each new work of actors already known from earlier scenes.

To the reappearing characters originating in *Le Père Goriot* the next work, *Un Drame au bord de la mer*, added three, all taken from *Louis Lambert* (Louis Lambert, Pauline de Villenoix, Lefebvre). They have nothing to do with the drama itself; it would lose nothing by omitting all reference to them. One cannot help surmising that the device of putting the story in the form of a letter from Louis to his uncle was an afterthought, inspired by Balzac's new idea of linking-characters. It illustrates the somewhat artificial methods to which he resorted to make his people reappear and the great importance which he attached to this technique.[2]

Melmoth réconcilié came next, a few months later (June 1835). It added three to the number of reappearing characters: Aquilina from *La Peau de chagrin*, and Frédéric and Delphine de Nucingen

---

[2] At about the same time, he used this device again — with perhaps more reason — in the almost witty letter by Natalie de Manerville to Félix de Vandenesse, at the end of *Le Lys dans la vallée*.

from *Le Père Goriot*. Unlike the three of *Un Drame au bord de la mer*, these had a direct contact with the action of the story, although Nucingen does not himself appear upon the scene.

Toward the end of 1835, *Le Contrat de mariage* and the beginning of *Le Lys dans la vallée* appeared almost simultaneously, though the Werdet publication of the latter as a whole was delayed until June 1836. In them the number of "new" reappearing characters was increased by seventeen, of whom three appeared first in the *Contrat* and reappeared in the *Lys*. It seems probable that the duc de Lenoncourt, the marquise de Listomère, Felix de Vandenesse, the marquis (his father), and perhaps Lady Dudley were created in *Le Lys dans la vallée;* but Natalie de Manerville in *Le Contrat de mariage*, as she has no part in the *Lys* itself (where she is brought in only by the device of her "correspondence" with Félix: cf. *supra,* note 2).

It would require considerable space to complete a detailed account of the gradual growth of the world which Balzac created by means of his technique of reappearing characters. Suffice it to say that, with publication of the concluding part of *L'Envers de l'histoire contemporaine,* the last work of Balzac to be printed before his death, the number of characters made to reappear *naturally* had reached a total in the vicinity of five hundred.

In the meantime, the other method of making characters reappear — the method of interpolating or substituting in new editions of works names which had originally been absent from them — had been industriously used and had not only vastly increased the number of reappearing characters in many stories (for instance, *Splendeurs et misères des courtisanes* has a grand total of some 190), but had actually added to their number, since in not a few cases the character does not reappear elsewhere. It is not possible to state arbitrarily an exact number for the full complement of reappearers in the *Comédie Humaine* (e. g., what to do about sundry unnamed clerks of Desroches, about numerous unnamed relatives of key personages, or even about the historical figures whom this monograph does not take into account?). By any set of criteria, however, a conscientious and thorough record of fictitious reappearers will include at least 550 names, but doubtless not as many as six hundred.

A few examples, despite solutions suggested here, will show further the unwisdom of reducing the reappearers either to rigid statistics or, in frequent instances, to theories about their origin in specific stories. —

1) The aname of Madame de Listomère appears first in *Le Père Goriot*. One cannot, however, help suspecting that this character already existed in the preliminary sketch of *Le Lys dans la vallée* when *Le Père Goriot* was being written. In *Goriot* she figures among such reappearers as Lady Brandon, the duchesse de Langeais, the comtesse de Sérisy and the comtesse de Kergarouët: save Madame de Listomère, no one is mentioned who was not already known to the reader from earlier stories. For Balzac she must also have been a reappearing character. That she was created in *Le Lys dans la vallée* seems all the more probable since she was the sister of Félix de Vandenesse, the hero of that story: in *Le Père Goriot* she has no other *raison d'être* than to help dress the aristocratic stage. From this we are justified in concluding that *Le Lys dans la vallée* existed in outline before the composition of *Goriot*. As early as March 1835, Balzac writes Madame Hanska: "Puis je prépare une grande et belle oeuvre, intitulée *Le Lys dans la vallée*." Again on May first, he refers to it as "sur métier".

2) Though the name of du Tillet had appeared in *L'Interdiction* before the publication of *César Birotteau*, one cannot doubt that the character was created in the latter work. In *L'Interdiction* he is alluded to (*Conard* VII, p. 149), but never comes on the scene.

3) The name "du Croisier" does not appear in *La Vieille Fille*, where this character is called "du Bousquier". Also, in *Les Petits Bourgeois*, this same personage bears the name of "du Bourguier".

4) In the original versión of *La Torpille*, Blondet is called "Alfred", not "Emile", as he had been in the first edition in *Le Cabinet des Antiques*, *La Maison Nucingen*, and *Une Fille d'Eve*. He was rechristened "Emile" in *Illusions perdues* (part II). As the character of the journalist was developed in that story, it strikingly recalled the description of Emile in *La Peau de chagrin*, and it may then have occurred to Balzac to merge the two by giving them the same name. Cf. Pommier, *Revue d'Histoire Littéraire*, L (1950), 192.

5) Though the name of Henry de Chaulieu first met the reader's eye in *Un Prince de la Bohême*, we must believe that the character was created in *Mémoires de deux jeunes mariées*. Here his family plays a central rôle, while in *Un Prince de la Bohême* there is merely

a casual reference to him (*Conard* XVIII, p. 382). The *Mémoires* had been projected long before and Balzac had worked on it at intervals since 1835, as shown by numerous references to it in letters to Madame Hanska. Under date of October 28, 1834, he wrote: "Je vais m'occuper des *Mémoires d'une jeune mariée*, délicieuse composition..." A month later: "*César Birotteau* avance et les *Mémoires d'une jeune mariée* sont sur le chantier." On January 16, 1835: "On m'offrait hier douze mille francs des *Mémoires d'une jeune mariée*."

6) A comparison of *La Fausse Maîtresse* and *Un Début dans la vie* leads to the conjecture that the vicomte de Sérisy was created in the latter, thougt the former was the first to appear. *La Fausse Maîtresse* came out in *Le Siècle* (five installments: December 24-28, 1841), and *Un Début dans la vie* in *La Législature* (twenty installments: July 26 — September 4, 1842). Balzac wrote his sister in February 1842: "*Les Jeunes Gens* ont fait un volume et je regarde cela comme une des perles de ma couronne." *Les Jeunes Gens* was the title provisionally given to *Un Début dans la vie* (yet, in *La Législature* it was called *Le Danger des mystifications*).

7) Cérizet and Petit-Claud were no doubt created in *Les Souffrances de l'inventeur* (= part III of *Illusions perdues*), as their names appear in the issues of *L'Etat* for June 11 and 16, 1843. Still, they are introduced without names in *Splendeurs et misères des courtisanes* in the issues of *Le Parisien* for June 18 and 20, 1843: in this novel their names do not appear until the *Furne* printing of 1844.

8) Though Madame Fontane's black hen is called "Bilouche" in *Les Comédiens sans le savoir* (*Conard* XIX, p. 349), Cléopâtre in *Le Cousin Pons* is surely the same black hen (*Conard* XVIII, pp. 60, 137). The lady's toad Astaroth keeps his same name in both stories (*Conard* XVIII, pp. 137, 204; XIX, p. 146).

9) Vinet, of *Pierrette* and *Le Cousin Pons*, was probably already in Balzac's unfinished *Petits Bourgeois* and *Député d'Arcis*, both of which he had certainly developed considerably in manuscript before the appearance of *Le Cousin Pons* in the spring of 1847. Note that in the *Furne edition* (XI [1844], p. 211) of *Les Employés*, Balzac refers the reader to *Les Petits Bourgeois* as if the latter were already an accessible part of the *Comédie Humaine*.

10) For the reader of *Une Ténébreuse Affaire*, *Le Député d'Arcis* and *La Cousine Bette*, there can be no doubt that Philéas Beauvisage belongs primarily — and probably originally — to *Le Député d'Arcis*. Cf. Lotte, pp. 29, 603.

CHAPTER III

GROUPING OF REAPPEARERS IN INDIVIDUAL
STORIES

The process of making a character reappear by changing the text of a work from which it was originally absent found its application particularly in the scenes completed before *Le Père Goriot*. That was the only way in which they could immediately acquire reappearing characters before their original characters could again be brought upon the scene in new compositions. The process, however, was not restricted to these works. In the revision to which Balzac subjected all the works for the Furne edition of the *Comédie Humaine*, which began to appear in 1842, the process was applied to almost every one, even to *La Fausse Maîtresse*, which was first published as late as December 1841. And if the process must be called artificial by comparison with the "natural" (cf. *supra*), it should not therefore be considered improper. As certain representatives of social groups became well known from their repeated appearances in the growing society of the *Comédie Humaine*, it would have been noticeable if they had failed to materialize in a work in which these groups are present.

In the salons of the Faubourg Saint-Germain, Madame Firmiani's for example, the princesse de Blamont-Chauvry, the marquise d'Espard, Diane de Maufrigneuse, Louise de Macumer were to be met as a matter of course; their absence rather than their presence would surprise us. But all these ladies were created after *Madame Firmiani* was written. The guests of the "amphitryon" in *La Peau de chagrin* (*Conard* XXVII, pp. 54 ff.) — notary, lawyer, vaudevilliste, doctor, land-owner, caricaturist, maker of ballads, journalist — who should they be but Cardot, Desroches, Cursy (du Bruel), Bianchon, Moreau de l'Oise, Bixiou, Canalis, Vignon? But some of these did not exist before 1842; not one of them existed before *Le Père Goriot*. In *La Femme abandonnée* (*Conard* IV, p. 258) the Blamont-Chauvrys, the Cadignans, the Grandlieus and the Navarreins were more likely, for the readers of the *Comédie Humaine*, to evoke the prestige of the old authentic nobility than the Soubises, the Lusignans and the Montmorencis; but Balzac did not supplant the latter until his annotations in his copy of *Furne*.

In *La Maison du chat-qui-pelote* (*Conard* I, p. 17) we cannot be surprised to see in the Guillaume salon the same persons — Camusot and Cardot, and the Birotteaus — whom we have seen together at the grand ball in *César Birotteau* (*Conard* XIV, p. 82). When in *Eugénie Grandet* (*Conard* VIII, p. 421) des Grassins becomes infatuated with "one of the prettiest actresses of the Théâtre de Madame," we find it quite natural that her name should be Florine. We have a clearer vision of the social world which Charles Grandet aspires to enter when it is the duchesse de Chaulieu, rather than the unknown duchesse de Margency, who has turned his prospective father-in-law's head (*Conard* VIII, p. 482). After reading *César Birotteau*, we are prepared to learn that the name of the landlord of Madame Crochard (*Une Double Famille*, *Conard* III, p. 236) is "Molineux" rather than "Rigolet".

Another reason for the appearance in the earlier stories of names not present at first is found in incidents in the lives of the original characters as developed in later works. In many cases where characters of the earlier stories had been made to reappear, so much had been revealed as to their identity or their fortunes that reference to this in the earlier stories became natural and sometimes almost necessary.

For example, Esther and Sarah van Gobseck could not be mentioned in the earlier editions of *Gobseck*, for Sarah was still to be created in *César Birotteau* and Esther in *La Torpille*. But after they had been created, they could not be completely ignored in the story of their rich relative, especially as he was to leave Esther his whole fortune (*Splendeurs et misères des courtisanes*, *Conard* XV, p. 333). In fact, the whole conclusion of *Gobseck* had to be rewritten, for originally Gobseck was still living at the end of the story, and there was no question of a will.[1]

In its first editions, *Une Double Famille* (cf. *Conard* IV, 299) could tell us of the daughters of the comte de Granville only that they were "richement mariées". After *Une Fille d'Eve*, it was only natural that the elder (Marie) had become comtesse de Vandenesse.[2] Of the count's sons, the first versions of *Une Double Famille* recorded merely that they had been successful; after the *Curé de village* and *Splendeurs et misères*, the Granville story could, and quite naturally did, tell us that "le vicomte, de Procureur-Général à Limoges, a passé Premier-Président à Orléans, et le cadet [Eugène] est ici, procureur du Roi."

After having learned from *La Cousine Bette* (*Conard* XVII, p. 376) that a younger brother of Alphonse de Montauran was still

---

[1] In her biographical notice of her brother (*EdDéf* XXIV, p. xl), Madame Surville is certainly in error in her explanation of the rewriting of *Gobseck*: "Il chercha longtemps un parti pour Mlle de Grandlieu, et rejetait tous ceux que nous lui proposions. 'Ces gens ne sont pas de la même société, le hasard pourrait seul faire ce mariage, et nous ne devons user que fort sobrement du hasard dans nos livres; la réalité seule justifie l'invraisemblance; on ne permet que le possible, à nous autres.' Il choisit enfin le jeune comte de Restaud pour Mlle de Grandlieu, et recomposa à cet effet la très-admirable histoire de *Gobseck*, où la plus haute moralité se trouve dans les faits et non dans les paroles." But Ernest de Restaud's attachment to Camille de Grandlieu and the prospect of their marriage are in the original version. It is precisely in view of this attachment that the story is told. One is tempted to risk the conjecture that Madame Surville was confusing the question of finding a suitable match for Camille with that of the marriage of the youngest daughter of Ferdinand de Grandlieu (*Splendeurs et misères des courtisanes*, *Conard* XV, p. 98). Apparently Juste de Grandlieu was created for this purpose. No mention of a son of Madame de Grandlieu occurs in *Gobseck* before the Furne edition. Indeed, his name is not mentioned in that edition, except for a reference to this projected marriage on the very last page. "Songez", says Madame de Grandlieu, "que mon fils sera quelque jour duc de Grandlieu, et réunira la fortune des deux maisons de Grandlieu." As the rewritten *Gobseck* appeared in 1842 (*Furne*), and *Splendeurs et misères* only in the following spring, it would appear that the latter novel must have been well advanced at least a year before its publication (after all, *La Torpille* had appeared as early as 1838). For the genesis and development of *Splendeurs et misères*, cf. the excellent (but unpublished) doctoral dissertation by Robert M. Strozier (University of Chicago, 1945).

[2] In *Une Fille d'Eve*, Miss Preston lists only 41 reappearers (plus a Galathionne not included by Balzac), whereas the novel brings in no fewer than 57.

living, and that Alphonse, "en mourant sous les balles des Bleus, avait confié les intérêts de son jeune frère au soldat de la République", the reader of *Les Chouans* could not have helped being puzzled had the end of the story not been changed; especially as in *Furne* and *Conard* the line just quoted is followed by "(Voir *Les Chouans*)."

In *La Femme supérieure*, which in *Furne* became *Les Employés*, Tullia is mentioned (*Conard* XIX, p. 86) only as a "danseuse plus remarquable par sa beauté que par son talent." After she had become the heroine of *Un Prince de la Bohême*, and after the story of her relations with the duc de Rhétoré had been told and these relations had become notorious in *Mémoires de deux jeunes mariées* (*Conard* I, p 190) and *Illusions perdues* (*Conard* XII, pp. 172, 256), some mention of them was almost called for in *Les Employés*. After the third part of *Illusions perdues* had been written, the name of Cérizet was almost of necessity inserted in the first part (*Conard* XI, 202); similarly, the first part needed Françoise de la Haye and Pierre Petit-Claud (pp. 261, 302).

It would be natural to expect that Balzac, once having used this device of interpolation and substitution to provide the stories before *Le Père Goriot* with reappearing characters, would have availed himself of every opportunity offered by new editions to exploit it. But the changes of this kind made before *Furne* are relatively few in comparison with the number resulting from the systematic exploitation of the process in that edition.

In the version of *La Maison du chat-qui-pelote* brought out in the Béchet edition (1835) of *Scènes de la vie privée*, there is only one substitution where there were eventually to be ten — that of Aiglemont for *le colonel* (*Conard* I, p. 63). In the other two stories in the same *Béchet* — *La* Vendetta and *Le Bal de Sceaux* — there were no substitutions, but in *Furne* there were 25 (increased to 28 in *EdDéf*).

In 1837 the fourth volume in *Scènes de la vie privée* was reprinted (by Werdet) with considerable changes in the text. Ronquerolles and Léontine de Sérisy replaced Flesselles and Madame de Roulay in *Le Rendez-vous;* Madame Firmiani was substituted for Madame Vitagliano in *La Femme de trente ans,* in which also the name of Madame de Listomère was interpolated (cf. *supra*). In the same year, in *La Grande Bretèche,* Horace Bianchon was substituted for M. de Vilaines and the name of Balzac's second-favorite doctor Desplein was interpolated, but the notary under whom Regnault had served his apprenticeship in Paris was still Chodron, and not Roguin as in *Furne* (also *Conard* VII, p. 412).

The Charpentier edition of 1839 offered opportunity for carrying much further the process of furnishing the pre-*Goriot* stories with reappearing characters. The fact remains, however, that Charpentier texts throughout the *Comédie Humaine* may be all but ignored, as important changes are nearly non-existent. By 1839, the society of Balzac's imaginary world had grown substantially with the appearance of *Le Contrat de mariage, Le Lys dans la vallée, L'Interdiction, La Vieille Fille, Illusions perdues* (parts I-II), *Les Employés, La Maison Nucingen, César Birotteau, Une Fille d'Eve*, and *Le Cabinet des Antiques*. Characters created in these novels had become familiar and had increased enormously the number of typical representatives of social groups which one might expect to encounter everywhere. But very few additions were made in *Charpentier* to the number of reappearing characters in earlier stories. In *Eugénie Grandet*, Roguin replaced the previously anonymous notary of Guillaume Grandet (cf. *Conard* VIII, p. 320). but none of this novel's other seven or eight substitutions found in *Furne* was made in 1839. In *Ferragus*, Antoinette de Langeais replaced an anonymous duchess, but none of the seven *Ferragus* characters interpolated in *Furne* was present in *Charpentier*.

Although the duchesse de Marigny (*Duchesse de Langeais, Conard* XIII, p. 287) is not a reappearing character, the substitution of her name for that of a duchesse de Valigny cannot pass unnoticed, as it is of particular interest for the study of Balzac's use of his device. It is only by accident, as it were, that there is no representative of the Marigny family among the reappearing characters. A "bois de Marigny" was mentioned in the first editions of *La Paix du ménage*, but became "bois de Navarreins" in *EdDéf* II, p. 420. In the first two editions of *Les Chouans* Alphonse de Montauran represented himself as the "marquis de Marigny", but in *Furne* and thereafter, his alias was "vicomte de Bauvan". Possibly with a view to a duchesse de Marigny in *La Duchesse de Langeais*, Balzac in *Modeste Mignon* makes mention of a Marigny family, explaining that Louis XIV "avait fait duc le marquis de Marigny". And this despite the *Chouans* "emendation" to a spurious vicomte de Bauvan. Furthermore, it should be remembered that a Madame de Marigny figured in the first editions of *La Paix du ménage,* but in *Furne* (I, p. 333) she became Madame de Grandlieu, and finally Madame de Lansac, in *EdDéf* (II, p. 417).

The result of Balzac's persistent application of his process in revisions for the Furne edition was to increase strikingly the size and significance of the group of reappearing characters in almost every work. The *Romans et Contes philosophiques* were the most refractory to his efforts. Many of these, like *Jésus-Christ en Flandre, L'Elixir de longue vie, Maître Cornélius, Les Proscrits, Sur Cathérine de Médicis (La Confidence des Ruggieri),* and *Le Chef-d'oeuvre inconnu,* have their action in earlier centuries, remote from the nineteenth-century world which the *Comédie Humaine* portrays. Still, only those just mentioned, together with *El Verdugo, Le Message, Le Réquisitionnaire,* and *Séraphîta,* remained without reappearing characters.

L'Enfant maudit, though more than two hundred years away from the *Comédie Humaine,* was given a distant relationship to it when a duc d'Hérouville appeared in *Modeste Mignon* (not to mention this name in *La Cousine Bette, La Muse du département, Le Cabinet des Antiques:* cf. Lotte, p. 283). When *L'Enfant maudit* was revised for *Furne,* the relationship in question was confirmed, inasmuch as Balzac changed to Grandlieu the name of the lady whom the duc d'Hérouville chose, after the tragic loss of both his sons, as the means of perpetuating his race. For further details, one should consult the sound and informative study by Jacob D. Isaac, *Variations between the successive editions of Balzac's "L'Enfant maudit"* (unpublished M. A. thesis, Chicago 1939): in particular, pp. 77-80.

In *L'Envers de l'histoire contemporaine* there is a Lecamus with forebears in the sixteenth century who had played capital rôles in Balzac's *Martyre calviniste.* However, further illustrations need not be multiplied to prove that Balzac was forever seeking to link even his stories from medieval times with any or all of the other great riches of his *Comédie Humaine.* His conscious grouping of reappearers in so many successfully revised individual stories gives every indication of what an additional twenty years of life would have yielded, — definitively.

CHAPTER IV

CHANGES DUE TO INTERPOLATION OR SUBSTITUTION OF NAMES

In the simplest form of interpolation Balzac merely inserted a name or names without otherwise altering the text, as in the following examples. The first sixteen of these involve the introduction or extension of lists.

Madame Firmiani: in *Furne* (I, 238) Balzac adds "par les Listomère, les Lenoncourt et les Vandenesse". Also in *Furne* (I, 241) he brings in a group including the marquise d'Espard, Louise de Macumer, and Diane de Maufrigneuse.

La Père Goriot: in the second Werdet edition of 1835 (I, 122), the list (cf. *Conard* VI, 256) is increased by the names of the duchesse de Carigliano, the comtesse Ferraud, madame de Lanty. In *Furne* (IX, 329), the following is added to this same list: "et la marquise d'Espard, la duchesse de Maufrigneuse et les Grandlieu".

César Birotteau: "les du Guénic" is added in *Furne* (X, 210) to a list already lengthy.

Le Contrat de mariage: addition in *Furne* (III, 277) of "madame d'Espard, les Nucingen".

La Duchesse de Langeais: in *Furne* (IX, 222) the dukes of Grandlieu and Maufrigneuse join the list.

Gobseck: in the Béchet edition (*Scénes de la vie parisienne*, I [1835], 239) Balzac introduced a list of historical figures not present in the three earlier versions, and in *Furne* (II, 380) he added the fictitious Kergarouët, Portenduère, and Simeuse.

Une Fille d'Eve: to the list of "ces femmes qui passent à travers

Paris comme les fils de la vierge dans l'atmosphère" are added (*Furne* II, 238) Coralie, Mariette, Suzanne du Val-Noble, Tullia.

Illusions perdues: in *Furne* (VIII, 122) Balzac creates a list by adding "les Blamont-Chauvry, les Lenoncourt" after "les Navarreins". Also in *Furne* (VIII, 359), a substantial list is populated further, by Victurnien d'Esgrignon.

L'Interdiction: in *Furne* (X, 153) a list is nearly doubled by the addition of Sixte du Châtelet, the marquis de Listomère, Maxime de Trailles, and "les deux Vandenesse" (Charles and Félix).

Les Secrets de la princesse de Cadignan: to the picture-gallery of the conquests by Diane de Maufrigneuse, Balzac adds in *Furne* (XI, 84) Victurnien d'Esgrignon, Alphonse de Rhétoré, and Ronquerolles.

La Vieille Fille (*Conard* X, 264): in *La Presse* (October 23, 1836) Balzac mentions a Blacas and an Avaray, who are still present in *Werdet* (*Scènes de la vie de province*, III [1837], 117). These are replaced in *Furne* (VII, 8) by the dukes of Lenoncourt and Navarreins. In his annotated *Furne* Balzac built these two names into a list of five, by adding Fontaine ("Grand-Jacques"), Flamet de La Billardière, and the ducal brother of Marie de Verneuil (*EdDéf* VI, 551).

La Maison du chat-qui-pelote: in a list more descriptive of its individuals than usual, Balzac added Madame Roguin and the silk-merchant Camusot (*Furne* I, 43). Cardot, the latter's father-in-law joined the list in *EdDéf* I, 28.

Le Bal de Sceaux: Balzac introduced (in *Furne* I, 138) a fairly formidable list, consisting of "les duchesses de Maufrigneuse, de Chaulieu, les marquises d'Espard et d'Aiglemont, les comtesses Ferraud, de Montcornet, de Restaud, madame de Camps et mademoiselle des Touches". Cf. *Revue d'Histoire Littéraire*, XLI (1934), 205-206.

In an interpolation consisting of three sentences, the Béchet edition (p. 279) introduces the following list into *Gobseck*: "Ne suis-je pas l'intime des Ronquerolles, des de Marsay, des Franchessini, des deux Vandenesse, des Ajuda-Pinto". This is the only mention of Franchessini outside of *Le Père Goriot*. In the first three printings of *Le Lys dans la vallée*, he figures with Lady Brandon, but their names were deleted in *Furne* (VII, 348).

Occasionally, in the process of adding new reappearing characters to the earlier stories to bring them into harmony with the rest of the *Comédie Humaine,* Balzac gave them a part in the action of the story. The conclusion of *Un Episode sous la Terreur* was completely changed in the 1842 version (published in *Le Royal Keepsake,* pp. 194-212): the details are given in *Conard* XXXVIII (1935), pp. 472-475. A less extensive revision involves the introduction of the chevalier de Valois in the Furne edition of *Les Chouans* (XIII, 50, 108, 121): he is not present in the earlier versions published by Canel and Vimont.

When, as in the greater number of cases, a character reappears by the substitution of a name for the one that was originally his, the replacement also may occur without further alteration of the text. Thus there is no other change in the text when in *Le Bal de Sceaux* Beaudenord, Manerville, and Palma are substituted for Sérisy, Montalant, and Brummer, when the marquis and marquise de Listomère replace an unnamed count and countess in *Etude de femme,* and when in *Une Doble Famille* Madame Chignard and Rigolet give way to Madame Roguin and Molineux. Indeed, considerably more than half of the substitutions are of this simple sort. Equally simple are the cases where the insertion of a name changes an anonymous character into a reappearing one. An excellent case in point is that of Taillefer's guests in *La Peau de chagrin,* as noted in the preceding chapter. In *Etude de femme* the narrator, greeted only as "mon cher" originally, becomes "mon cher Horace" in the revision and is thus identified with Horace Bianchon. The insertion of the names was sufficient to change Guillaume Grandet's broker and notary into Roguin and Souchet (*Eugénie Grandet*), and "un brocanteur" into Elie Magus (*La Vendetta*).

But in numerous cases the matter is not so simple, and the change of character invites or compels considerable changes in the text. Here are a few examples:

1) At the beginning of *Gobseck,* Camille de Grandlieu is being warned about marriage to Ernest de Restaud, because he has "une mère qui mangerait des millions, une femme mal née, une demoiselle Goriot qui jadis a fait beaucoup parler d'elle. Elle s'est si mal comportée avec son père qu'elle ne mérite certes pas d'avoir un si bon fils." Earlier, this had read merely: "Ernest a une mère qui mangerait dix millions".

2) In *Le Bal de Sceaux*, the difficult Emilie de Fontaine is explaining her objections to various possible husbands: " 'Qu'as-tu à dire contre M. de Rastignac?' - 'Madame de Nucingen en a fait un banquier', dit-elle malicieusement" (*Conard* I, 98). Prior to *Furne* the text read "Saluces" instead of "Rastignac", and Delphine de Nucingen was introduced only in *EdDéf* I, 92.

3) In *Le Bal de Sceaux*, the following passage from the first edition (Mame et Delaunay-Vallée, *Scènes de la vie privée*, I [1830], p. 338): "Un soir, Emilie étant sortie à cheval avec son oncle, qui depuis les beaux jours avait obtenu de sa goutte une assez longue cessation d'hostilités, ils rencontrèrent la calèche de la vicomtesse (*Abergaveny*, mentioned p. 336). Cette fois c'était bien l'étrangère. Elle avait pour compagnon un gentlemen (*sic*) très-prude et très-élégant dont la fraîcheur et le coloris, dignes d'une jeune fille, n'annonçaient pas plus la pureté du coeur qu'une brillante toilette n'est un indice de fortune. Hélas! lex deux étrangers n'avaient rien dans leurs traits ou dans leur contenance qui pût ressembler aux deux séduisans portraits que l'amour et la jalousie avaient gravés dans la mémoire d'Emilie". *Conard* I, 110: "Un soir, Emilie, sortie à cheval avec son oncle, qui depuis les beaux jours avait obtenu de sa goutte une assez longue cessation d'hostilités, rencontra lady Dudley. L'illustre étrangère avait auprès d'elle dans sa calèche monsieur Vandenesse. Emilie reconnut ce beau couple, et ses suppositions furent en un moment dissipées come se dissipent les rêves".

4) In *Les Chouans*, in the Vimont edition (1834), I, p. 334: " 'Cet homme en veste déchirée qui appuie tous les doigts de sa main droite sur le panneau comme un pacant', dit mademoiselle de Verneuil en riant.—'Vous l'avez, pardieu, deviné. C'est un ancien contrebandier' (this reply is spoken by Alphonse de Montauran).—'*Et son voisin, celui qui serre en ce moment sa pipe de terre blanche*'.— '*C'est l'ancien garde-chasse* (italicized words not in the Canel edition of 1829) du défunt mari de cette dame' ".—*Conard* XXII, 166: " 'Cet homme en noir qui ressemble à un juge?'—'C'est un de nos négociateurs, La Billardière, fils d'un conseiller au parlement de Bretagne, dont le nom est quelque chose comme Flamet; mais il a la confiance des princes'.—'Et son voisin, celui qui serre en ce moment sa pipe de terre blanche, et appuie tous les doigts de sa main droite sur le panneau comme un pacant', dit mademoiselle de Verneuil en riant.—

'Vous l'avez, pardieu, deviné, c'est l'ancien garde-chasse du défunt mari de cette dame' ".

In the examples so far given, the person who is rechristened to become a reappearing character is only mentioned or, if brought upon the stage, is only a supernumerary and makes but a momentary appearance. But in a few instances the substitution affects a more important actor. Then the changes made necessary in the text are greatly multiplied, and it happened now and then that Balzac nodded in his work of revision and neglected to make them. In *La Paix du ménage,* Montcornet was substituted for "le colonel". Although Montcornet is a count and a general, the original "colonel" is still left unchanged no fewer than nine times (*Conard* III, pp. 318, 323, 325, 330, 331, 333, 337, 339, 341): cf. also William B. Hart, *Variations in the printed versions of Balzac's 'La Paix du ménage'* (unpublished M. A. thesis, Chicago 1939), pp. 72-76. In *Madame Firmiani,* the comte de Valesnes (one of the three principals in the story) was changed in *Furne* to Monsieur de Bourbonne; but the revised text still keeps a trace of the evicted nobleman where (*Conard* III, 370) it is "le comte" and not Bourbonne who replies to Madame Firmiani. In *La Duchesse de Langeais* the duc de Grandlieu supplanted the marquis de Cassan, but in the scene between this individual and the duc de Navarreins, Balzac overlooked one place where the change of title needed to be made, and we read (*Conard* XIII, 288): " 'Vous savez pourquoi?' répondit le marquis, en jetant au duc un fin sourire". In *Le Rendez-vous* the marquise de Belorgey disappeared and was replaced in *Werdet* (1837; p. 38) by la comtesse de Listomère-Landon, but Balzac failed to remove a clue to her former identity when he left uncorrected the line (*Conard* VI, 26): "Avant d'arriver au salon, la marquise avait déjà, suivant l'habitude des provinces, commandé à déjeuner pour ses deux hôtes".

CHAPTER V

CHRONOLOGICAL INCONSISTENCIES IN THE *COMÉDIE HUMAINE*

It would seem that every teller of a story must have a constant concern for the time-element in the sequence of the events that he relates, and thus the story must have in the mind of the author a definite chronology. This, however, may be more or less carefully worked out in detail according to the nature of the interest and according to the author's desire to produce the illusion of reality; it may go to the point of being scrupulously adjusted to the calendar, as for instance in Hardy's *Return of the native* and in the minute chronology of the thirteenth-century *Roman de Flamenca*.

It would be natural to expect that Balzac, intent as he was on giving to his tales a stamp of authenticity, would be as careful about details in time as he was about those of place and material environment. In his work the omnipresence of dates, often very precise, confirms this expectation. We are told with considerable exactness not only how much time is covered in each story, but how that time is distributed by seasons and months.

In sixteen stories, the very opening words fix the starting point by reference to year, if not more narrowly to season or to month, or even to day. This is the more striking if we consider that Balzac's method of presenting his characters in close dependence on their social and material environment made him primarily concerned with setting his stage, elaborating his background, creating his *milieu*, before introducing his action. It should be pointed out, however, that only *Gambara* and *Un Episode sous la Terreur* begin by specifying the day of the month, and that in none of the sixteen incipits in question is the day of the week added: consequently, we cannot test the harmony of the date with the actual calendar. In spite of the omnipresence of dates in the stories, which leave us seldom in uncertainty as to the movement of the action in time and which mark its progress from year to year and season to season and month to month and even day to day, the exact combination of day of the month, day of the week and year, is very hard to find. We might expect to find it in *Mémoires de deux jeunes mariées,* an epistolary novel composed exclusively of letters. But curiously enough they are often dated only by the month, without day or year, and when both day and year are entered, there is nothing to permit the reader to refer such dating to a day of the week.

I have found only four cases in the *Comédie Humaine* which might afford an answer to the question whether Balzac carried his chronological conscientiousness to the point of consulting the calendar. One of these is in *Une Double Famille,* two are in *Un Début dans la vie,* and one in *Modeste Mignon.* In *Modeste Mignon,* the day following an eventful Sunday in October 1829 is referred to as the 17th, but in 1829 the 17th of October was a Friday. In *Une Double Famille,* Caroline Crochard, in 1816, "dans les premiers jours du mois de mai, un samedi matin qu'elle apercevait une faible portion d'un ciel sans nuages, dit à sa mère: 'Maman, il faut aller nous promener demain à Montmorency' ". The excursion was made, and on that Sunday began Caroline's romance with the mysterious man in black who was in reality the comte de Granville. Six years later the anniversary is celebrated; the day is the sixth of May—a Sunday, as the calendar confirms. In *Un Début dans la vie* there are two *procès-verbaux* in which the waggish Godeschal records the celebration of Desroches' accession to his *étude* and that of Oscar Husson's reception as junior clerk. One is dated "ce dimanche, 27 juin", and the other "aujourd'hui lundi, 25 novembre". Both dates are from 1822, in which, however, June 27th was not Sunday but Thursday, while November 25th was really Monday. Balzac is then right twice out of four times. Is this good guessing or careless consultation of the calendar? Of course, the matter is of no consequence save as a measure of the degree of methodical care that Balzac gave to factors of time in the structure of his novels.

There is another way of assessing the amount of attention Balzac gave to his chronology. It is to examine in detail all of the multitude of dates and time-measures which help to give the illusion of accurate reporting of real events, and thereby to ascertain whether they harmonize and combine to make up a consistent time-schedule—a Calendar that is at least true to itself. One doest not have to go far in this direction to discover a degree of uncertainty, in spite of the imposing array of precise dates and exact noting of the passage of time. In *La Fausse Maîtresse*, for instance, the opening sentence gives the date of the marriage of Clémentine du Rouvre as September 1835, but a little further on the date becomes December 1835 instead.

Readers of *César Birotteau* will remember the hectic days immediately preceding the fatal fifteenth of January on which the perfumer's bankruptcy was declared and his frantic efforts to avoid that catastrophe. Beginning on the thirteenth, César has interviews with five individuals from whom he seeks help, and also journeys to Nogent-sur-Marne and Sèvres: all this in two or three days the dating of which is confused in all versions of the novel. A somewhat similar case occurs in *Modeste Mignon*, where a precisely timed series of events leads up to a hunting party to begin on an eighth of November, but here again the sum of incidents exceeds the total allowed by Balzac's dating. Further illustrations are to be found in at least fifteen further stories. Also, I suppose there are at least twenty-five examples of disparities involving birth-dates, each in one and the same story.

A feature that is rather incompatible with the acceptance of a studied and systematic chronology in the *Comédie Humaine* is the changing of dates from one edition to another. Such changes are extremely frequent, and the incompatibility is emphasized when we notice that the alterations do not add to the coherence and consistency of the time-sequence, but frequently diminish or destroy it, as in the example just cited from *César Birotteau*.

Take the case of *Eugénie Grandet*. In the Béchet edition (October 1833) Eugénie meets her cousin Charles on her birthday, November 17, 1819. Charles Grandet's father, ruined by the dishonesty of his business agent, has just committed suicide and Charles is setting out for the Indies to seek his fortune. Eugénie's mother dies in 1820, her father in the last days of 1825. Charles returns in June 1826. Eugénie's agent in Paris, des Grassins, presently learns that Charles is back, and goes to tell him about the state of his father's affairs, and also about the death of his uncle and aunt. Eugénie and her father had managed to stave off the creditors so as to save the family name from the stigma of bankruptcy. Charles cynically declares his unconcern, and writes to Eugénie to break their engagement; she receives the letter at the beginning of August. On the heels of this letter comes another from des Grassins reporting his interview with Charles, who, he says, had reached Paris a month before. All this is quite consistent. But in *Furne,* while the starting date remains the middle of November 1819, Eugénie's mother dies in 1822 instead of 1820, her father in 1827 instead of 1825; Charles returns in 1827 instead of 1826, albeit before instead of after the death of Félix Grandet. Charles has been in Paris six months instead of one when des Grassins calls on him, though the latter's letter still says that he had returned one month before. Besides this last inconsistency, there is the difficulty of supposing that Charles would have gone six months with no knowledge of what had happened in his uncle's family and that des Grassins, constantly occupied with Charles's creditors, would have been for six months ignorant of his presence in Paris.

Or take this case in *Le Curé de village.* In the *Souverain* text of 1841, Sauviat went to Paris in December 1821 to prepare the way for the marriage of his daughter Véronique. In the February following, the marriage preparations are under way, and occasion an outburst of gossip in Limoges. In *Furne* Balzac changes December 1821 to December 1822, but the February date remains unchanged, and we have the gossip nearly a year before Sauviat's journey to Paris.

A change in *Un Début dans la vie* brings Balzac's story into conflict with the course of nature. In the *Dumont* edition (1844) the ruin of Clapart occurs in 1803; he does not survive the shock and dies leaving his wife *enceinte.* The child, Oscar, is born in 1804. In *Furne* 1803 is changed to 1802, but the date of Oscar's birth remains the same. I doubt whether medical annals record a parallel case.

In *Les Secrets de la princesse de Cadignan,* the date of the marriage of Diane d'Uxelles to the duc de Maufrigneuse was originally 1815, when she was seventeen. In *Furne* it was 1814, but Diane was seventeen regardless. Originally, her son Georges was born in 1817, being eighteen in 1835: in *Furne* he was nineteen in 1833, the date of 1835 having been changed, and accordingly was born at least one year too soon. Aside from the slight confusion, why did Balzac take the trouble to vary these two dates?

The chronological incoherences and inconsistencies so far presented occur within the framework of one and the same story. Their number might be considerably augmented. They are, however, immediately multiplied when we consider all the stories of the *Comédie Humaine* and compare them together, as we must, connected as they are by the device of reappearing characters. By making each separate story a part of the larger whole Balzac immensely complicated the chronological problem, and made something like a fixed and detailed chronological chart a matter of necessity if he was to avoid discrepancies and contradictions among the different stories. The multitude of such discrepancies and contradictions as reveal themselves upon examination would seem to afford positive evidence that Balzac never worked to such a chart.

Let us start with dates given us by the biographies of his characters. He seldom leaves us in ignorance of the age of his personages, and he gives them with an air of exactness. Rarely does he content himself with the merely approximate by using an *environ*. And more frequently he avoids the round numbers that do not seem to have quite the precision of the others. His personages are 79, or 63, or 27, rather than 80 or 50 or 25. But when we compare their ages in different stories, we are not always referred to the same year of birth. The writer du Bruel was born in 1796 in *La Rabouilleuse* and in 1790 in *Un Prince de la Bohème*. Eléonore de Chaulieu was born in 1773 on one page of *Modeste Mignon* and in 1779 on another, but in 1785 in *Mémoires de deux jeunes mariées*. Desroches was born in 1796 in *Un Début dans la vie* and in 1795 in *La Rabouilleuse*. Florine was born in 1805 in *Illusions perdues* II, in 1806 in *Une Fille d'Eve*. The comte de Fontaine died in 1824 in *Les Employés*, in 1828 in *La Muse du département*. Emilie de Fontaine was born in 1796 in *Une Fille d'Eve*, in 1803 in *Le Bal de Sceaux*. Marie Gaston (son of Lady Brandon) was born in 1809 in *Mémoires de deux jeunes mariées*, in 1810 in *La Femme abandonnée*. In *L'Illustre Gaudissart* the "hero" was born in 1793, but in 1794 or 1796 in *César Birotteau*. Esther van Gobseck was born in 1805 in *La Torpille*, in 1806 in *La Rabouilleuse*. Clotilde de Grandlieu was born in 1802 in *Splendeurs et misères des courtisanes*, in 1805 in *Béatrix*. In *La Vendetta* (Mame and Béchet editions) Fanny

Planta is the leader of the liberal group among the pupils of Servin in July 1815; she does not act nor talk like a child of thirteen; but when she became Mathilde Roguin in *Furne*, that age was given her, since we know from *Pierrette* that Mathilde was born in 1802.—"J'en passe et des meilleurs", among them Marsay, that prime favorite of Balzac among all the creatures of his imagination, who figures in no fewer than thirty different tales; he was born in 1792 if we believe *La Fille aux yeux d'or,* or in 1796, or in 1798 if we believe *Autre Etude de femme.*

In another category of discrepancies I may cite the following. In *Le Cabinet des Antiques* we learn that Camusot was promoted from his provincial position to the judicial bench of Paris at the begining of 1825, whereas in *La Dernière Incarnation de Vautrin* his wife says in May 1830: "Nous ne sommes à Paris que depuis deux ans". In *César Birotteau* Flamet de la Billardière is *chef de division* in 1818, when he is invited to the grand ball; in *Les Employés* he did not become *chef de division* until 1822 or 1823. Also in *César Birotteau,* Crottat succeeded Roguin as notary in 1819; in *Les Paysans* Amaury Lupin is sent by his father from Burgundy to Paris "chez maître Crottat, notaire" in 1814. In *César Birotteau* the crash and flight of Roguin occurs in the very last days of December 1818, but this was introduced into *Eugénie Grandet* as the cause of Guillaume Grandet's suicide in November 1819. In *La Rabouilleuse,* three days after the Roguin disaster, a draft for a thousand francs drawn by Philippe Bridau in New York is presented to his mother; Joseph, her other son, manages to get the money to pay the draft in ten days; a week after that a letter comes from Philippe to say that he is just leaving New York for Le Havre; Madame Bridau "courut au-devant de son fils bien-aimé; le paquebot arriva par une belle matinée du mois d'octobre 1819"; the story says nothing of how she endured the intervening months. In *Le Contrat de mariage* Elie Magus was called in to appraise the jewels of Madame Evangélista in Bordeaux in 1822, but in *Pierre Grassou* Magus, "venu de Bordeaux, débitait à Paris" in 1819. Also in *Le Contrat de mariage* Marsay writes to Paul de Manerville in November 1827, informing him of the recent death of the father of the brothers Vandenesse; in *Un Début dans la vie* the Vandenesse succession was in litigation in 1825. In *La Rabouilleuse* Florentine makes her début at the Opéra in April 1823, but in *Un Début dans la vie* she had not yet reached this point in 1825. In *La Maison du chat-qui-pelote* the duchesse de Carigliano in 1813 was a woman of thirty-six, but in the *Député d'Arcis* her father was not married until 1795. In *La Duchesse de Langeais* Antoinette flees from Paris to the refuge of the convent in Spain in the summer or early fall of 1819; in *Le Père Goriot* she is at Madame de Beauséant's ball February 16, 1820. I might go on almost indefinitely, if I were cruel enough to empty my 200-odd *fiches* upon the reader.

Occasionally Balzac was apparently aware of such discrepancies and changed his chronology to avoid them. Some of the many changes of date may have been due to such a consideration, though we do not detect the reason. But when, in the *Furne* revision of *Une Double Famille*, he changed the rupture of the liaison of the comte de Granville and Caroline Crochard from 1827 to 1824, we can see a reason for it in the fact that in *La Torpille* Carlos Herrera (Vautrin) has established Esther van Gobseck in the apartment which Caroline had occupied but which she can no longer keep up. In *Béatrix* the date of du Halga's return to his old home in Guérande was changed from 1814 to 1824, for the former date was no longer consistent with his appearance in *La Bourse* as an habitué of Madame de Rouville's apartment in 1818.

In the earlier stories, before the end of 1834, the chronology is not infrequently thrown out of adjustment by the introduction of characters from other tales or by the identification of original characters with those of other tales by means of a change of name. In *Gobseck* the *avoué*, in 1816, was only *second clerc* in the office of maître Bordin and did not succeed him to become independent until 1819. Balzac seems to have been conscious of the difficulty, for in revising *Le Colonel Chabert* he moves the opening scene in the office of the former *avoué* (now Derville) from 1817 to 1818, a change which does not quite resolve the discrepancy. Indeed, he made it even more harsh by yielding to the temptation to connect *Le Colonel Chabert* also with *César Birotteau*: this involved a reference, as of May 1818, to the Roguin failure noted above.

An examination of the chronology in *Illusions perdues* will perhaps give us a further glimpse into Balzac's labor of composition. The first part of the novel ends with Lucien de Rubempré installed in a cheap lodging in the Latin Quarter, his funds precariously depleted, himself abandoned by his protectress (Louise de Bargeton), without friends, alone. The chronology offers no dificulty; it is simple and consistent. The only hint of trouble is found in a change of date made in the *Furne* revision of the story, a change which at once destroys the consistency. In the *Werdet* versión (1837) Sixte du Châtelet, exploiting his superior knowledge of Paris for its effect on Madame de Bargeton, says to her: "Demain j'aurai sans doute une loge à quelque spectacle". Balzac adds by way of explanation: "Au mois de septembre les ministres ne savent que faire de leurs loges aux théâtres..." In *Furne* Balzac changed the September (1821) to June The only possible explanation is that he realized, when *Illusions perdues* was complete, with the addition of its second and third parts, that there was something wrong with the chronology. The second part (*Un Grand Homme de province à Paris*) runs originally from September 1821 to the following June. The succession of events is not precisely fixed in the calendar, but is fairly clear and offers scant difficulty. In May Lucien is driven to forge three drafts for a thousand francs each, but the proceeds hardly suffice to pay his debts. Before the end of June 1822, his mistress Coralie dies. At the end of his resources, Lucien turns back home to Angoulême.

The third part (*Eve et David*) begins with Lucien's return. Apparently when Balzac began writing *Illusions perdues* III, the time of this journey from Paris was June or July. In Angoulême Lucien receives almost immediately an invitation from du Châtelet (who had married Louise de Bargeton in 1821) for September 15, 1822. Balzac could not fail to see the contradiction which this date involved and, in revising *Illusions perdues* II for *Furne,* he sought to bring it into harmony by prolonging Lucien's Paris struggles and by postponing the death or Coralie to the last of August 1822. But curiously, in a chronological confusion which is hard to explain, Balzac interposed another two months between Coralie's death and Lucien's death, so that, as we follow now step by step the passage of time in *Illusions perdues,* we find Lucien leaving Paris at the end of October and arriving in Angoulême about September first.

The reason for transferring the beginning of *Eve et David* from June to August is to be found in the development of the incidents imagined by Balzac for this concluding part of *Illusions perdues.* As he worked out the details of the plot, he saw that Lucien needed much more time —for redeeming his forgeries of May 1822— than the period until the following September. Consequently, Balzac changed the date of the forgery to the tenth of February. His choice of the tenth is puzzling, as also the statement in a staggering bill presented to David Séchard on May fourth to the effect that the due-date was April thirtieth. In any case, Balzac finally (and perhaps with sagacity) leaves this chronological matter *dans le vague*.

The inference from the foregoing pages is manifest and inescapable. The chronology in the *Comédie Humaine* is confused, loose, and unstable; and it excludes utterly the supposition that Balzac ever worked out something like a fixed and definite calendar to which the events narrated in his stories could be referred. When he assigned ages to his characters as they reappeared, he was not relying on a written record but upon his memory or upon his intimate knowledge of a given personage, just as he would assign an age to his neighbors and friends. And what effect, if any, does this have on our impression of Balzac? Do we not wonder rather that, in all the welter of the multitudes acting their parts in the *Comédie Humaine* and in the tangle of their individual rôles, he should have been so nearly right? Does it not give us new evidence of the marvelous grip of his imagination on the world of its creation? Does it not illumine and confirm the idea, often repeated but often skeptically received, that for Balzac these men and women who peopled that world were real and living, more living and real than his own frends and neighbors? That he knew them better than he knew the men and women with whom he dined and did business and conversed, to whom he seemed so often like a man dazed, living in a world apart?

CHAPTER VI

FURTHER INCONSISTENCIES AND CONTRADICTIONS

Legitimate as was the process of interpolating and substituting characters in stories already completed before 1835, it was subject to evident limitations. The reappearing person must not be given a rôle that is out of character with what we already know of him. He may not appear at a place where he could not well have been, because in another story he is represented as having been in some other place at that time. And he may not, without arousing the reader's skepticism, be introduced into an action definitely fixed in time in such a way as to be doing at a given moment something which, in another story, he had done at a different time. The reappearing persons must meet the demand of consistency in character, place and time. As the preceding chapter implies, it is in the matter of time that Balzac most frequently failed to satisfy this demand.

A comparison of *Gobseck, Le Père Goriot, Le Colonel Chabert,* and *César Birotteau* reveals the difficulties that Balzac encountered when his project for reappearing characters led him to make Madame de Restaud a daughter of Goriot and to identify Madame de Grandlieu's legal adviser with Derville (the narrator in *Gobseck*). When Balzac made Madame de Restaud confess, in February 1820, the shameful pass to which her infatuation for Maxime de Trailles had brought her and her pawning of the family diamonds, he apparently forgot that in *Gobseck* the episode of the diamonds happens in 1816. When he came to revise *Gobseck* for *Furne,* he removed this inconsistency by changing the dates in that story. But if this change brought *Gobseck* into harmony with *Le Père Goriot,* it created an equally flagrant inconsistency with *Le Colonel Chabert*, because this change postponed until 1819 the moment when Derville succeeded Bordin, and at least until 1820 the moment when he became the successful advocate of Madame de Grandlieu. In *Le Colonel Chabert*, however, Derville originally was established as *avoué* by 1817, and the case of Madame de Grandlieu was not yet decided. Perhaps it was the recognition of this inconsistency that led Balzac to change the dates in *Le Colonel Chabert*. Originally the time of Chabert's first call at Derville's office is February 1817, to which date the internal evidence of the narrative also points. But changing the year[1] to 1818 evidently does not remove the contradiction. Furthermore, by introducing in *Béchet* (p. 307) the notary Crottat, "ce jeune homme qui venait d'acheter l'étude où il était maître clerc, et dont le patron venait de prendre la fuite en faisant une épouvantable faillite", Balzac created an inconsistency between *Le Colonel Chabert* and *César Birotteau*. Crottat appears in Derville's office in May 1818: Roguin's bankruptcy and Crottat's succession to his business did not occur, in *César Birotteau*, until the end of that year (cf. *supra*).

Another typical instance of the chronological difficulties into which Balzac was in danger of running when he introduced characters into works in which they did not originally belong is found in *Etude de femme*. The death of the comtesse de Mortsauf is mentioned in *Furne* (and hereafter) as current news; the action of *Etude de femme* cannot be placed before 1829, for Rastignac and Madame de Listomère talk about the opera *William Tell* which had its first performance in that year; yet, according to *Le Lys dans la vallée*, Henriette died in 1820. We can hardly believe that, even in that day of slow communications, it took nine years for news from the provinces to reach the newspapers of Paris.[2]

In *Une Double Famille* the comte de Granville, in November 1805 is encouraged by a powerful member of the government to hope for political advancement. "Vous avez fort bien plaidé certaines causes embrouillées", he tells him, in the versions prior to *Furne*. In the revision Balzac's desire to bring in his reappearing characters made him see here an opportunity to introduce the

---

[1] Cf. Juanita K. Bromberg, in *Dargan-Weinberg*, p. 388.
[2] Cf. *Revue d'Histoire Littéraire*, XLI (1934), 206, note 2.

Simeuse and Hauteserre brothers whose story had been told in *Une Ténébreuse Affaire*. So he changed the minister's words and made him say: "Vos défenses dans le procès Simeuse et d'Hauteserre vous ont placé bien haut." But Balzac left the date, November 1805, standing, although the trial of the brothers had not taken place until 1806.

In the *Furne* revision of *Illusions perdues* II the name of Victurnien d'Esgrignon is interpolated in the list of royalists who congratulated Lucien de Rubempré on deserting his liberal friends and coming over to their side. This was in March 1822, but in *Le Cabinet des Antiques* the young Esgrignon did not even leave Alençon until the end of that year.

Julie d'Aiglemont had no children other than Hélène until the different parts of *Même Histoire* were brought together by the *Furne* substitution (1842) of the Aiglemont name for those of Vieumesnil, Verdun, and Cassan. But in *Ursule Mirouët*, which appeared in *Le Messager* in 1841, Madame d'Aiglemont is represented as seeking the hand of Ursule in 1833 for her eldest son. The overture seems a little premature since her eldest son, if she had one, could not be older than fifteen (her eldest child, Hélène, having been born in 1817). The marriage would have been somewhat ill assorted, since the husband would have been so much younger than the wife; Ursule was nineteen at that time.

Shortly before Easter in 1825, as we learn in *Le Bal de Sceaux*, the comte de Fontaine urged his daughter Emilie to make a choice among the various possible aspirants to her hand. One of these, in the *Mame* and *Béchet* editions, was a certain Montalant. When Balzac's eagerness to multiply his reappearing characters led him, in revising the story for *Furne*, to substitute Paul de Manerville for Montalant, he apparently forgot that Paul already had a wife, having in *Le Contrat de mariage* married Natalie Evangélista in 1822. And why should the comte de Fontaine think of Paul de Manerville, whose hair is black (*Conard* VII, p. 215), when one of the reasons Emilie gives for rejecting the proposed suitor is that he is blond and she does not like blonds (*Conard* I, p. 98)? And when in *Le Bal de Sceaux* Balzac, substituting Lady Dudley and Félix de Vandenesse for the vicomtesse Abergaveny and her unnamed companion, made them appear repeatedly in Lady Dudley's carriage, did he forget that in *Le Lys dans la vallée* Félix had solemnly protested to

Natalie de Manerville in 1827 that his relations with Lady Dudley had ceased immediately after the death of Madame de Mortsauf (1820), and that from that day on he had not met Arabella except on formal social occasions?

In *La Duchesse de Langeais*, Madame François Keller, by substitution for a Madame Bouvry, appears as a bride in 1818, but in *Le Député d'Arcis* we are told that her son Charles was born in 1809.

When, in *Furne*, the comte de Kergarouët and the chevalier du Halga entered *La Bourse*, replacing the anonymous benefactors of Madame de Rouville, a contradiction of dates resulted between this story and *Béatrix*. In the latter novel, in which du Halga first appeared, he had been mayor of Guérande throughout the period of the Restoration, yet at the same time in *La Bourse* he was a regular visitor of Madame de Rouville in Paris. Balzac apparently noticed this contradiction, because the *Béatrix* text was changed in *Furne;* in the revised version du Halga did not return to Guérande until the death of Louis XVIII and had been an habitué of the du Guénic salon not for twenty but for fifteen years. But even fifteen yeas was too many, for the death of Louis XVIII occurred in 1824 and the action of *Béatrix* begins in 1836.

In *L'Auberge rouge* the mother of Joséphine Mauricey is still living after 1830, according to the versions in the *Revue de Paris* (XXIX [August 1831]) and in the Gosselin edition of *Nouveaux Contes philosophiques* (1832). In *Le Père Goriot* Victorine Taillefer's mother had been dead for several years before 1819. When Joséphine Mauricey became Victorine Taillefer in the *Werdet* revision (1873) of *L'Auberge rouge*, Balzac removed the glaring contradiction by making her the step-daughter instead of the daughter of the Madame J.-F. Taillefer of that moment, and made other emendations in the text to reconcile the stories,[3] but without getting rid of the difficulties arising from the fact that ten years separate the actions. Joséphine Mauricey in becoming Victorine Taillefer became at once ten years older, but she does not betray her age: she seems even younger than the Victorine of *Le Père Goriot*. Perhaps it was to conceal this difference of time that Balzac emended the opening phrase of *L'Auberge rouge* from "vers la fin

---

[3] Cf. Ruth B. Dunn, in *Dargan-Weinberg*, pp. 380-381.

de l'année 1830" to "en je ne sais quelle année", but if this concealed it did not change the time of the action in *L'Auberge rouge,* and the contradiction still persisted. A consistency between *L'Auberge rouge* and *Le Pére Goriot* can be attained only at the cost of a new contradiction between *L'Auberge rouge* and *La Peau de chagrin.* If the death of Taillefer, which is announced in the funeral notice *(L'Auberge rouge)* as having occurred on May first, be supposed to have happened earlier than 1831, he could not have given in October 1830 the sumptuous banquet described in *La Peau de chagrin.*

By interpolating a reference to Jacques Falleix in *Les Employés* *(Furne* XI, p. 260) and also in *Ferragus (Furne* IX, p. 107), Balzac brings these two stories into conflict. In *Ferragus* Jules Desmarets sells his business to Jacques Falleix early in 1819. In *Les Employés* it is not until 1824 that Martin Falleix "établit son frère agent de change".[4] — Also in *Les employés (EdDéf* XI, p. 112), Savinien de Portenduère was added to the group of "célébrités" frequenting the salon of Madame Rabourdin in 1824, but according to *Ursule Mirouët* he could have been only eighteen years old at that time.

In *La Fausse Maîtresse* Balzac describes the house bought by Adam Laginski in 1834. It had been built by a rich Englishman, probably in 1831 or 1832. When Balzac substituted Steinbock for Gérard-Séguin *(EdDéf* II, p. 474), who had been named in the earlier editions as one of the artists who had contributed to its elaborate decoration, he apparently forgot that in 1833 Steinbock had not yet begun his apprenticeship to the arts *(Cousine Bette).*

In *La Rabouilleuse (Conard* IX, pp. 320 ff.) Philippe Bridau, in December 1821, is living at home in Issoudun, down at the heels, shabby, stealing from his brother and aunt the sums which he squanders on gambling and drink. In *Illusions perdues* II *(Conard* XII, pp. 244, 266) he appears at about the same date, by the interpolation of his name in *Furne* (VIII, pp. 303, 320), among dinner-guests in Paris.

Mariette, substituted for Madame de Valmonzey in *César Birotteau (Furne* X, p. 350), is made to appear along with Florine as an actress of established reputation in 1818, although according to

---

[4] Cf. *Papers of the Michigan Academy,* XII (1929), 272-273.

La Rabouilleuse, in which she was created (*La Presse,* installment of February 28, 1841), Mariette was only fourteen at that time and did not make her début until 1820.

Discrepancies, whether psychological or physical, between two persons merged by the process of substitution are more difficult to detect and measure than the inconsistencies of time and place. Each of them must have been described in such detail as to give the character a distinct personality. Physical incompatibilities are more readily detected than psychological ones. It is easy to see the contradiction between a Paul de Manerville with black hair in *Le Contrat de mariage* and a blond Paul de Manerville in *Le Bal de Sceaux* (cf. *supra*). It is more difficult to say that a given speech or act attributed to one character could not equally have been spoken or performed by the other. A person may appear on the scene, engage in conversation, and have a part in the action, but say nothing and do nothing that could not quite as well have been said and done by a dozen others. Balzac frequently changed the names of the parties to a conversation. In the *Furne* revision of *La Torpille,* he put in the mouth of Montcornet a remark originally given to Finot, attributed to Vernou words of Blondet, to Lousteau a speech of Vernou, and to Nathan one of Couture. In *Autre Etude de femme* Balzac, in the second edition,[5] made Canalis contribute to the conversation the judgement on Napoleon which in *Furne* (II, p. 448) had been pronounced by Daniel d'Arthez, although one would hardly have expected these two to formulate their ideas about Napoleon in the same terms. While Balzac did not change anything in the words of the opinion, he did recognize the difference between the speakers and modified the phrase by which it is introduced: instead of "dit Daniel d'Arthez en laissant échapper un geste naïf", he wrote "dit Canalis avec un geste et un accent emphatiques."

La Femme de trente ans offers the most striking example of the disastrous results that could follow when this process of substitution was exploited without the necessary precautions and beyond the inescapable limitations.[6] It is only too evident that, in spite of the unity created by the common subject, the six (or seven) episodes do

---

[5] *La Lune de miel, II* (published by Chlendowski, 1845), p. 261.
[6] Cf. *supra,* chapter I; *Revue d'Histoire Littéraire,* XLI (1934), 212-214; Maurice Bardèche, *Balzac romancier* (texte abrégé: Paris, 1943), pp. 260-267.

not present a single group of persons; that in each episode the group is formed in view of a certain aspect of this common subject; and that it is the subject rather than the individual actors that makes of them one "même histoire".

To make it plausible to regard the several stories as episodes in the life of one and the same family, it would have been necessary to do more than change a few dates. And even so far as dates go, Balzac did not realize the confusion and contradictions that were going to result from the changes, or else was unwilling to undertake the amount of work that would have been necessary in order to avoid them. Except in the last chapter, only one change in date was made; four years were taken from the age of Madame d'Aiglemont. This was very far from making the parts fit together as one whole. The attempt to arrange the events of the different chapters in a consistent time sequence ends in failure.

The tragic dénouement of the first episode occurs in the winter of 1823, but in the following chapter Madame d'Aiglemont, now twenty-six years old, has taken refuge with her daughter in the castle of Saint-Lange "vers la fin de l'année 1820". She leaves Saint-Lange in October of the next year. In the third chapter, Charles de Vandenesse meets her on the eve of the Congress of Laibach (Ljulbjana, January 1821), yet four years are to have elapsed since the end of the first episode. Thus, to be consistent with *Le Rendez-vous*, the action in *A Trente Ans* would have to be changed, at the earliest, to late 1826.

For the opening scene of the next-to-last chapter, no date is indicated in the text. Madame d'Aiglemont is now thirty-six years old (Madame de Verdun had been forty before *Furne*). She has besides Hélène and Gustave two other children: Moïna, seven years old, and Abel, ten. For consistency with *La Vallée du torrent*, we must suppose this scene to have occurred in 1841; and, since *Les Deux Rencontres* requires six years, the action cannot end before 1847.

Originally the final chapter begins in early June 1832, but this date was changed to 1841 in *Furne* and to 1844 in *EdDéf*. The latter date was evidently still at least three years too early to achieve consistency. Madame d'Aiglemont is fifty years old, but she was thirty-six in 1841; the time of this last episode is thus fixed as 1855. To say nothing of postdating Balzac's own death, this date is in distinct contradiction with other years mentioned in the chapter. Gustave, born in 1828, was said originally to have been killed in the Spanish campaign of 1823, and Abel was supposed to have met his death in the July revolution, 1830. To change the date of Gustave's death to 1832 and that of Abel to 1836 did not really help matters at all, for Gustave was still living in *Les Deux Rencontres*, in 1841; and Abel was only an infant, if indeed already born, at the time of the battle of Macta in 1835. Gustave was marquis at the time of his death and so appears to have succeeded to the title several years before his father's death.

No two chapters of *La Femme de trente ans* are consistent with each other, much less all six (or seven). When they are compared, contradictions start up at every turn. From the moment when Balzac made the Aiglemont name reappear throughout the stories, confusion reigned. Our considered judgement must surely be that Balzac was right in his preface of 1835 and that, when he yielded to the temptation to apply his device of reappearing characters to *Même Histoire*, he became the victim of his system, and that the stories thus tied together in *La Femme de trente ans* would gain rather than lose if their original independence were restored to them.

CHAPTER VII

NUMBER AND IMPORTANCE OF INDIVIDUAL REAPPEARANCES

So far we have considered only the processes and the difficulties through which, step by step, the number of reappearing characters was increased. Now we must examine results of these processes from points of view other than that of the number of reappearers. Many names among them are not familiar to the general reader of Balzac; some, indeed, are so unfamiliar that even the devoted admirer would be at a loss to recall a given character, the stories in which he is found and the rôles he plays in them. Our recognition of a name is due to one or both of two possible causes: either it has occurred frequently in various stories, or the character has played such a significant part in one that we do not forget. So, the reappearances of a character are to be measured quantitatively by their number and qualitatively by the extent of his or her participation in the action of a given story.

Of the 550-600 reappearing characters, some 225 reappear but once. But these single reappearances must not always be dismissed as unimportant or perhaps even accidental. Some of them are indeed due to the fact that a later story returns to the scene of an earlier one. The following pairs of stories are so closely related as to account for many of the single reappearances: *Illusions perdues* and *Splendeurs et misères des courtisanes; La Vieille Fille* and *Le Cabinet des Antiques; Les Employés* and *Les Petits Bourgeois; Une Ténébreuse Affaire* and *Le Député d'Arcis*. While in more than half of the cases of single reappearance, the returning character has no other function to perform than just to "reappear", such characters become only the better witnesses for Balzac's devotion to his technique, better even than a dozen reappearances of a character within the pairs of stories just noted. Nothing else but his conscious purpose to multiply reappearers and reappearances could have prompted Balzac, at the expense of many flagrant inconsistencies, to substitute Bourbonne (*Curé de Tours*) for Valesnes (*Madame Firmiani*), to make Madame d'Aiglemont propose her son Gustave as a suitor for the hand of Ursule Mirouët, to choose the vicomte de Granville in spite of his extreme youth to be the prosecutor of Jean Tascheron in *Le curé de village*, to substitute Mathilde Roguin for the leader of the liberal group in Servin's studio (*La Vendetta*), to have the Sorias (imported from *Mémoires de deux jeunes mariées*) write the letter that informs the duc de Chaulieu of the death of his son-in-law in *Splendeurs et misères* I, to "discover" in a hitherto anonymous soldier of *Les Chouans* the major Brigaut created in *Pierrette*, to make Coloquinte (from *Illusions perdues* II) a survivor (in *La Rabouilleuse*) of the famous charge of Colonel Chabert, to have Alain (in *L'Envers de l'histoire contemporaine*) make the only reference to Benassis outside of *Le Médecin de campagne* itself, to make Félix de Vandenesse (in *Le Lys dans la vallée*) mention Madame Evangélista who appears elsewhere only in *Le Contrat de mariage*, to choose the parents of Alexandre Crottat as the victims of La Pouraille near the end of *Splendeurs et misères*, to include Moïna de Saint-Héreen among those who conspire against the comtesse Félix de Vandenesse (*Une Fille d'Eve*), or to cite Franchessini among the friends of Maxime de Trailles (*Gobseck*).

To measure the reappearances qualitatively we must consider the rôle, greater or less, which the reappearing characters play. They fall into three main groups: in the first (*I*) the reappearing characters have no part in the action of the story; in the second (*II*) they play a significant secondary rôle; in the third (*III*) they are principals in the action. In the first group we may distinguish (*Ia*) those who are merely mentioned but never actually appear; (*Ib*) those who appear but are silent onlookers, as it were, supernumeraries; and (*Ic*) those who have a speaking part of a purely incidental sort that does not in any considerable way affect the action or involve their distinct individuality. Categories such as those defined here are, of necessity, frequently arbitrary, and lines of demarcation are often only vaguely drawn.

The most conspicuous examples of category *Ia* are to be found in the many mere lists which Balzac delighted to multiply. His lists were often designed to give the world of Balzac's imagination an air of authenticity comparable to that of the real world. Frequently, in fact, he made substitutions in which historical figures gave way to lists of people created in the *Comédie Humaine*. Category *Ib* is also largely populated by means of lists, notably of guests at balls, dinners, receptions. Characters in *Ic* may utter no more than a single remark or be quoted from a letter or otherwise; a few are narrators, such as Bixiou in *La Maison Nucingen*, Desroches in *Un Homme d'affaires*, Bianchon in *La Grande Bretèche*, but — unlike Félix de Vandenesse who is both narrator and a principal in *Le Lys dans la vallée* — these individuals do not participate in the central action.

Also in *Ic* belong essentially the individuals who reappear in the salon of Félicité des Touches in *Autre Etude de femme* (cf. *infra*) and listen to Marsay's tale of his first romance and contribute to the ensuing conversation in which Balzac worked over the earlier *La Femme comme il faut*. Here the interest is evidently not in the characters themselves but in the ideas not originally nor necessarily even characteristically theirs. In this connection, we recall the remark by Canalis which had been given earlier to Arthez (cf. *supra*, chapter VI). If the characters in *Autre Etude de femme* are known and familiar, it is not in the interest of the story or of the discussion, but to give an impression of unity and reality to the world of the *Comédie Humaine*. This may also be said of the many reappearers in *La Femme-auteur*, the brief fragment which Balzac began in 1847, and similarly in *Mademoiselle du Vissard*. Just as in his last years, many more instances adorn — and sometimes disfigure — almost all the stories that preceded *Le Père Goriot*.

Of the three main categories just discussed, the first is by far the largest, containing about five-sixths of all reappearances. Only about once in ten times does a reappearing character play an individual and characteristic part which could not have been played by another quite as well. That is only what we should expect from Balzac's avowed purpose. That purpose was not to give a completer development and realization to the creations of his imagination, although he did that with Vautrin and Lucien de Rubempré and Rastignac, nor to exploit his characters by making them give new exhibitions of their individual talents, although he did that too in a few instances (Bixiou, Lora, Contenson, Trailles, La Palférine), but to give the reader a conviction of the unity and reality of the world which the various *Scènes* of the *Comédie Humaine* so richly portrayed.

APPENDIX A

Professor Canfield's frequent references, in Chapter I, invite further clarification concerning *La Femme de trente ans*, the more so as bibliographical data about this "novel" are still incomplete and often obscure (notably in connection with the Béchet and Werdet printings of volume IV of *Scènes de la vie privée*). For example, certain references in Dargan-Weinberg (pp. 64, note 229; 95, note 387; 183) fail to show that the University of Chicago library has this volume only in the Werdet edition, an edition not mentioned in Lovenjoul, Bardèche, or Conard. In 1933, Professor Canfield pointed out (*MLN* 48: 497) that this text "really makes a fourth edition of *Même Histoire*", one for which Balzac claims to have made "de grands changements par rapport au sens général" of the novel. From Professor Canfield's records and from the notes in *Allem* (cf. *infra*), it is clear that none of these changes concern the names for reappearing characters.

The first publication in which all seven sections of the story appear together was issued under the title *Même Histoire*, filling the complete fourth volume of the Béchet *Scènes de la vie privée* (September 1834: pp. 13-398). This is also the first publication anywhere to include sections II and IV*b* (*Souffrances inconnues* and *La Vallée du torrent*). The novel is preceded by a preface which was dropped from *Werdet* and from subsequent editions; for the text, cf. *EdDéf* XXII (1872), 382-384. Also, *Béchet* does not yet include a passage which, important to Balzac, is introduced in *Werdet* (250^8-251^8) and preserved without significant variants in *Conard* (150^{1-22}). Professor Canfield's records imply, accurately, that elsewhere *Werdet* yields no divergence of consequence from the Béchet printing.

La Femme de trente ans, as a collective title for the complete novel, is introduced for the first time in *Furne*. In *Mame* and in *Werdet*, there is no collective title, so that each text has the aspect of offering a group of short stories. A foreword at the beginning of *Mame* indicates that Balzac rejected the title *Esquisse d'une vie de femme*. In *Béchet* and *Charpentier* the collective title is *Même Histoire*.

The continuingly disorganized manner in which *La Femme de trente ans* came to be assembled into the alleged form of a single novel suggests varying procedures for anyone's classification of its reappearing characters. For example, Aiglemont, the principal name in the story, which is already in *Revue*^{2} (cf. *infra*) for section I, is not mentioned in any text of section II, replaces "Vieumesnil" after *Charpentier* in section III, is always absent from section IV*a*, is introduced by *Furne* into section IV*b* where the principals had been previously without surnames; the "Verdun" of section V becomes anonymous in *Furne* (until just at the end), and the "Ballan" of section VI gives way in *Furne* to "Aiglemont" throughout. As another example, the father of Charles de Vandenesse, who is mentioned only as "son père" in all the editions (cf. Conard VI, 135): before *Furne* the name "Vandenesse" is never in section IV*b*.

Section by section, the patch-work which is *La Femme de trente ans*, is accounted for in the bibliographical tabulation which follows (providing, incidentally, a key to the notations in the four preceding paragraphs).

I. *Premières Fautes.*

> *Revue*[1]. — *Caricature* (November 25, 1830), pp. 27-30. Corresponds to *Furne* 3^{10}-10^4; *Conard* 5^{23}-15^3; *Allem* 5^{10}-14^{12}. Fragment in *Revue*[1] published under title *La Dernière Revue de Napoléon.*
> *Revue*[2]. — *Revue des Deux Mondes*, III (September 1831), 517-555; IV (October 1831), 74-109. Corresponds to *Conard*, 3-41 and 42^3-80^{12}, respectively. Title in *Revue*[2] is *Le Rendez-vous.*
> Mame (—Delaunay). — *Scènes de la vie privée*, IV (1832), 5-158. Title is *Le Rendez-vous.*
> Béchet. — *Scènes de la vie privée*, IV (1834), 13-149. Title is *Le Rendez-vous.*
> Werdet. — *Scènes de la vie privée*, IV (1837), 1-131. Title is *Le Rendez-vous.*
> Charpentier. — *Scènes de la vie privée*, II (1839, 109-209. Title is *Le Rendez-vous.*
> Furne. — *Comédie Humaine*, III (1842), 1-61. Definitive title: *Premières Fautes.*
> EdDéf. — III (1869), 521-584.
> Conard. — VI (1912), 3-80.
> Allem. — (1944), 3-79.

II. *Souffrances inconnues.*

> Béchet, 153-190.
> Werdet, 132-170.
> Charpentier, 210-239.
> Furne, 61-78.
> EdDéf, 584-603.
> Conard, 80-102.
> Allem, 80-102.

III. *A Trente Ans* (before *Furne*, title is *La Femme de trente ans*).

> *Revue*[3]. — *Revue de Paris*, XXXVII (April 1832).
> Mame. — *Scénes de la vie privée*, IV (1832), 161-207.
> Béchet, 193-234.
> Werdet, 171-212.
> Charpentier, 240-272.
> Furne, 78-97.
> EdDéf, 603-623.
> Conard, 103-127.
> Allem, 103-127.

APPENDIX A

IV. *Le Doigt de Dieu.*

This chapter, published as a single unit in *Furne* and thereafter, contains two episodes formerly entitled *Le Doigt de Dieu* (or *La Bièvre*, as in *Béchet, Werdet, Charpentier*) and *La Vallée du torrent*. These are numbered here as IV*a* and IV*b*, respectively.

> *Revue*[4]. — *Revue de Paris*, XXIV (March 25, 1831), 233-239. Contains only IV*a*.
> *Mame*, 211-224. Contains only IV*a*.
> *Béchet*, 237-250, 251-263.
> *Werdet*, 213-225, 226-238.
> *Charpentier*, 272-283, 283-292.
> *Furne*, 97-103[18], 103[22]-109.
> *EdDéf*, 623-629[32], 629[36]-636.
> *Conard*, 127-135[14], 135[19]-142.
> *Allem*, 128-135[24], 135[29]-142.

V. *Les Deux Rencontres.*

> *Revue*[5]. — *Revue de Paris*, XXII (January 21 and 28, 1831), 216-244, 282-304. Does not include the final pages (*Conard*, 197[25]-200[35]) which, from *Mame* through *Charpentier*, form a separate chapter entitled *Enseignement*.
> *Mame*, 227-338.
> *Béchet*, 267-367.
> *Werdet*, 239-333.
> *Charpentier*, 293-365.
> *Furne*, 109-153.
> *EdDéf*, 636-683.
> *Conard*, 142-200.
> *Allem*, 143-198.

VI. *La Vieillesse d'une mère coupable* (before *Furne*, title is *Expiation*; *L'Expiation* in *Mame*).

> *Mame*, 341-372.
> *Béchet*, 371-398.
> *Werdet*, 334-361.
> *Charpentier*, 366-387.
> *Furne*, 153-165.
> *EdDéf*, 683-696.
> *Conard*, 201-207.
> *Allem*, 199-214.

APPENDIX B

As originally written by Professor Canfield, the present monograph included tabulations for all stories in *Furne* (I-XVIII) in which reappearing characters were introduced. While the serviceability of such a record for Balzac investigators is inestimable, it is not economically practical to include it here. However, this final chapter would be incomplete without at least two of the tabulations which Professor Canfield began many years ago. As his text indicates, *Autre Etude de femme* has special illustrative interest: his unpublished notes show similar preoccupation with Balzac's procedure in the three sections of *Béatrix*. From the tabulations which follow, the reader may appraise the usefulness of two Balzac mediocrities as a key to his habits of revisión during a period (1832-1844) which cuts very fairly across the best of his career.

In these tabulations, AEF = *Autre Etude de femme*, B = *Béatrix*, GBr = *La Grande Bretèche*, MD = *La Muse du département*, L indicates a character mentioned only in list(s), asterisks indicate characters mentioned but not by name, figures in superscript denote line-numbers, and references for *Revue* are given by date rather than by page. Other abbreviations are accounted for in the bibliographical notes below, or else on p. xii *supra*.

BÉATRIX (1839, 1844)

Location of B in the editions.

Part I. — *Les Personnages.*

> *Revue.* — *Le Siècle* (1839): 13 installments appearing each day from April 13 to April 26 inclusive, except for April 24. Title is *Béatrix, ou Les Amours forcés.*
> *Souverain.* — *Béatrix, ou Les Amours forcés* (2 vols., 1840): I 23-323 (= *Conard* 3-124^{24}); II 1-33^3 (= *Conard* 124^{25}-138).
> *Furne.* — III (1842) 285-388^{11}.
> *EdDéf.* — III (1869) 157-267.
> *Conard.* — V (1912) 3-138.

Part II. — *Le Drame.*

> *Revue.* — *Le Siècle* (1839): 10 installments appearing each day from May 10 to May 19 inclusive.

Souverain (cf. *supra*). — II 33⁴-298 (= *Conard* 139-254).
Furne. — III (1842) 388¹²-476.
EdDéf. — III (1869) 267-361.
Conard. — V (1912) 139-254.

Part III. — *Un Adultère rétrospectif.*

Revue. — *Le Messager* (December 24, 25, 26, 31; January 4, 5, 7, 8, 11, 12, 14, 15, 16, 17, 21, 22, 23: 1844-1845).
Chlendowski. — *La Lune de miel* (2 vols., 1845): I 5-324 (= *Conard* 255-343⁷); II 5-110 (= *Conard* 343⁸-376).
Furne. — IV (1845) 1-94.
EdDéf. — III (1869) 361-461.
Conard. — V (1912) 255-376.

For Part I of *B*, see Joachim Merlant, *Revue d'Historie Littéraire*, XX (1913), 602-636. For Parts II-III, see Brucia H. Dedinsky, *Variations between the first and the final editions of Balzac's 'Béatrix'* (unpublished M. A. thesis, Chicago 1926), pp. 40-52.

CLASSIFICATION OF REAPPEARING CHARACTERS

Since nearly six years separate the composition of *B* I-II from that of *B* III, the novel thus divides itself into two units for which the reappearing characters are classified accordingly. The tabulation for *B* I-II includes all first mentions in Part I (*Conard* 3-138) and in Part II (*Conard* 139-254); but, in cases where the tabulation shows only one reference, the character in question was introduced by Balzac in one part and not in the other. It will be noticed that reappearing characters are utilized in *B* I-II with about the normal emphasis which one would expect from Balzac in 1839, but this technique is rarely applied as concentratedly as in *B* III, where old acquaintances assemble in virtual "town meeting" (as also, for instance, in *La Maison Nucingen* and *La Femme-auteur*).

Reappearing Characters in B I-II.

Characters who first appear either in *B* I or in *B* II.

Ia   Casterán (comte de; brother of Béatrix) 96.
Kergarouët (vicomte de) 36.
Rochefide (Arthur de) 95.

Ic   Du Guénic (baronne Calyste; née Sabine de Grandlieu) 251.
Note that in *Revue* and *Souverain* her name is "Clémentine", but "Sabine" thereafter.
Du Halga 39, 149.
Grandlieu, Sabine de. Cf. *supra*, Du Guénic.

APPENDIX B 53

II   Conti (Gennaro) 62, 140.
     Du Guénic (baron; father of Calyste) 18, 148. Note the spelling *Guaisnic* (*Conard* 10-11), and see Merlant, *loc. cit.*, p. 605.
     Vignon (Claude) 81, 139.

III Castéran, Béatrix de. Cf. *infra*, Rochefide.
     Des Touches (Félicité; = "Camile Maupin") 35, 139.
     Du Guénic (Calyste) 18, 139.
     Rochefide (marquise Arthur de; née BÉATRIX de Castéran) 95, 140.

Characters who antedate *B* I and *B* II

Ia   *Ajuda-Pinto (Miguel d') 95.
     *Ajuda-Pinto (première marquise d') 95.
     Beauséant (Claire de) 237.
     Blondet (Emile) 109.
     *Cambremer (Jacques) 198.
     Cambremer (Pierre) 198.
     Castéran (marquis de; father of Béatrix) 96.
     Castéran (Marquise de; mother of Béatrix) 96.
     Ferdinand 60.
     Fontaine (Emilie de) 48, 163.
     Fontaine ("Grand-Jacques") 48.
     Kergarouët (amiral de) 39, 163.
     Kergarouët (comtesse de; the admiral's first wife) 192.
     Langeais (duchesse de) 237.
     Lenoncourt (duc de; father of Henri) 46.
     Lousteau (Etienne) 109.
     Montauran (Alphonse de; = "le Gars") 60.
     Montcornet (Virginie de) 96.
     Nathan (Raoul) 102.
     Rastignac (Eugène de) 116.
     Rochefide (father of Arthur) 96.
     Vandenesse (Charles de) 48, 163.

Ib   Grandlieu (duchesse Ferdinand de) 251.

     Reappearing characters not in the first printing but present in later editions.

Ia   *Ajuda-Pinto (seconde marquise d') 251; *EdDéf* 258.
        Not in *Revue* V-19; *Souverain* II 290; *Furne* 473.
     *Grandlieu (Athénais de) 251; *EdDéf* 358.
        Not in *Revue* V-19; *Souverain* II 290; *Furne* 473.
     Grandlieu (Juste de) 251; *EdDéf* 358.
        Not in *Revue* V-19; *Souverain* II 290; *Furne* 473.
     Grandlieu (mademoiselle de) 251; *EdDéf* 358.
        Not in *Revue* V-19; *Souverain* II 290; *Furne* 473.
     (N. B.—Like *Souverain* and *Furne*, *Revue* V-19 does refer to *two* Grandlieu daughters, but Sabine is the only one of the five sisters who is named specifically in any printing before *EdDéf*.)

Portenduère (amiral de) 40; *Furne* 313.
"Comte d'Estaing", *Revue* IV-15; *Souverain* I 112.
Verneuil (duc de; father of Marie) 129; *EdDéf* 259.
  Not in *Revue* IV-25; *Souverain* II 11; *Furne* 381.
*Verneuil (Marie de) 129; *EdDéf* 259.
  Not in *Revue* IV-25; *Souverain* II 11; *Furne* 381.

Ib   Grandlieu (Clotilde de) 251; *EdDéf* 358.
        Not in *Revue* V-19; *Souverain* II 290; *Furne* 473.
      Hannequin (Léopold) 252; *Furne* 474.
        Not in *Revue* V-19; "le notaire", *Souverain* II 292.

Reappearing Characters in B-III.

(N. B.—Persons already referred to in *B* I or in *B* II are listed in italics in the following tabulation for *B* III.)

Characters who first appear in *B* III

Ia   Cadine (Jenny) 320.
      Stidmann 330.
      Vissembourg 335. As noted on this *Conard* page, Vissembourg's younger brother is the "prince de Chiavari, le fils cadet du feu maréchal Vernon". Lotte (p. 117) indicates that these relationships are explained in *La Cousine Bette*, but Balzac's only reference either to Chiavari or to Vernon is the one in *B* III, as cited here.

Ic   Brossette (abbé) 311.

Characters who antedate *B III*

Ia   *Ajuda-Pinto (première marquise d')* 318.
      (L) *Ajuda-Pinto (seconde marquise d')* 338.
         Antonia 327.
      (L) *Argaïolo (duchesse d')* 276.
         Arthez (Daniel d') 278.
      (L) *Beaupré (Fanny)* 320.
         *Beauvisage (Cécile) 338. Despite Lotte's hesitations (pp. 30, 603), there seems to me no doubt that she is the comtesse de Trailles.
         *Beauvisage (Philéas) 338.
         Bixiou (Jean-Jacques) 330.
         Blondet (Emile) 335.
         Blondet (juge) 335.
         Chaulieu (Henri de) 310.
         Chaulieu (Louise de). Cf. *infra*, Macumer.
         Conti (Gennaro) 263.
         Du Bousquier 334.
         Du Bruel (madame). Cf. *infra*, Tullia.

APPENDIX B 55

    *Du Ronceret (madame la présidente) 331.
    *Du Ronceret (président) 331.
    Du Val-Noble (Suzanne) 320.
    Esgrignon (Victurnien d') 325.
    Espard (marquise d') 346.
  (L) Florentine 320.
    Florine 320.
  (L) *Fontaine (Emilie de)* 338.
    Grandlieu (vicomtesse de; mother of Juste) 292. This character cannot be Athénais, who is still unmarried at p. 308.
    Grindot 275.
    La Bastie (madame de). Cf. *infra*, Mignon.
    La Baudraye (Dinah de) 356.
  (L) Laginski (Adam) 325.
  (L) La Roche-Hugon (Martial de) 325.
  (L) Lenoncourt-Givry (duchesse de; née Madeleine de Mortsauf) 276.
  (L) Lenoncourt-Givry (younger brother of Louise de Macumer) 276
    L'Estorade (Renée de) 258.
    Macumer (Louise de) 258, 310.
    Malaga 320.
  (L) Mariette 320.
    Maufrigneuse (Berthe de) 276.
    Maufrigneuse (Diane de) 278.
  (L) Maufrigneuse (Georges de) 276.
    Mignon (Modeste; = madame de La Bastie) 338.
    Mortsauf, Madeleine de. Cf. *supra*, Lenoncourt-Givry.
  (L) Nucingen (Augusta de) 338.
  (L) Restaud (Camille de) 338.
    Rhétoré (Alphonse de) 276.
  (L) Ronquerolles 325.
    *Rubempré (Lucien de) 274.
    *Trailles (comtesse de). Cf. *supra*, Beauvisage.
    Tullia (= madame du Bruel) 330.
    Vernisset (Victor de) 330.

Ib   Du Tillet (Ferdinand) 342.
    Finot (Andoche) 328.
    Grandlieu (Juste de) 256.
    Lora (Léon de) 330.
    Lousteau (Etienne) 330.
    Rastignac (Eugène de) 325.

Ic   Ajuda-Pinto (Miguel d') 310.
    Canalis (Melchior) 277.
    Couture 330.
    Des Touches (Félicité; = "Camille Maupin") 258.
    Du Halga 263.
    Galathionne 326.
    Gobenheim 329.
    Grandlieu (Athénaïs de) 256.
    Grandlieu (Clotilde de) 255.
    Grandlieu (Ferdinand de) 256. Quoted, p. 317.

56   THE REAPPEARING CHARACTERS IN BALZAC'S "COMÉDIE HUMAINE"

       Marsay (Henri de) 290. Quoted.
       Mirouët (Ursule) 291.
       Nathan (Raoul) 277 (see also p. 359).
       Portenduère (Savinien de) 276.
       Vignon (Claude) 328.

II   Du Ronceret (Fabien) 331.
       Grandlieu (duchesse Ferdinand de) 255.
       La Palférine (Charles-Edouard de) 330.
       Rochefide (Arthur de) 316.
       Schontz (Joséphine) 317.
       Trailles (Maxime de) 298.

III   *Du Guénic (Calyste)* 255.
       Du Guénic (baronne Calyste; née Sabine de Grandlieu) 255.
       Rochefide (marquise Arthur de; née BÉATRIX de Castéran) 260.

       Reappaering character not in the first printing but present in later editions.

Ia   Nucingen (Frédéric de) 325; *EdDéf* 420.
       "Rothschild", *Revue* I-12; *Chlendowski* I 266; *Furne* 56.

In *Béatrix* the character of Félicité is not interestingly developed; Béatrix achieves only too well the comprehensive mediocrity which Balzac intends; Calyste is colorless throughout, as is Sabine, except for her letters in the early pages of *B* III. Balzac's description of Guérande, and especially of the du Guénic château, yields some charming paragraphs. Conti and Vignon are convincing and, in different fashion, so is Calyste's father, whereas his mother is rather too good to be true.

According to the above tabulation, 102 characters may be regarded as reappearers in *Béatrix*; of these, 20 appear both in *B* III and before. Miss Preston's total for this novel is 66.

As Miss Dedinsky has pointed out (thesis, p. 40), Balzac hit upon the name "Rochefide" toward 1843; the previous name, "Rochegude", appears only in the printings of *B* I-II, but not in the editions after *Furne*.

A list (*Conard* 96) includes the families of Esgrignon, Troisville, and Verneuil. The Navarreins family was also mentioned here in the earlier editions (*Revue* IV-20, *Souverain* I 253, *Furne* 356), but not in *EdDéf* 232. Where *Conard* 163 and *Furne* 406 read "Ces Kergarouët sont-ils parents des Portenduère et du vieil amiral de Kergarouët", the earlier editions (*Revue* V-11; *Souverain* II 91) have "Charlotte de Kergarouët est-elle parente du vieil amiral de Kergarouët".

The marriage of Suzanne du Val-Noble is alluded to in *B* III (*Conard* 327), but her husband, Théodore Gaillard (listed by Miss Preston as a *Béatrix* reappearer), is not mentioned.

Mindful of the canon of scholarly completeness, one notes that "Mistigris" (*Conard* 42) is merely the jack of clubs in a pack of cards, and not the familiar nickname of reappearer Léon de Lora.

Balzac introduces several lists in *B* III, and in all cases the editions agree, from *Revue* to *Conard* inclusive. In *Conard* these appear on pp. 276,

320, 325, 327, 338, 347, 348; also, the various characters in *Conard* 330 are already present in *Revue* I-15.

Other novels are mentioned in *B* III, but these allusions scarcely allow of addition(s) to the *Béatrix* list of reappearing characters: *Un Début dans la vie* (*Conard* 323), *La Fausse Maîtresse* (*Conard* 320), *La Femme abandonnée* (*Conard* 277), *Une Fille d'Eve* (*Conard* 320).

* * *

AUTRE ETUDE DE FEMME (1842)

Location of *AEF* in the editions.
Furne. — II (1842) 423-457.
Chlendowski. — *La Lune de miel* (2 vols., 1845): II 117-303. Title is *Premières Armes d'un lion*.
EdDéf. — IV (1869) 525-562^{36}.
Conard. — VII (1913) 361-406^{29}.

It is essential to remember that in *EdDéf* (562^{37}-583^{1}) and *Conard* (406^{30}-430^{21}) the story of "La Grande Bretèche" (*GBr*) is included —without separate title or other mark of chapter división— as the final part of *AEF*. *GBr* appears in *Furne* (IV 95-112) as a chapter by itself, but Balzac's final intention was to have it incorporated into the text of *AEF*. The *GBr* story is, however, such a distinct unit in its own right that Professor Confield was well justified in his decision to have its few reappearing characters tabulated apart. It is, of course, his procedure which is retained here. Furthermore, *GBr* was published several times between 1832 and 1845, without being in any way linked to *AEF*.

Future research on *AEF* and *GBr* will benefit substantially from the study by William L. Crain, *The Reworking of Balzac's 'Autre Etude de femme'* (unpublished M. A. thesis, Chicago 1925). His dissection of the text and of its several transformations in Balzac's lifetime is minutely thorough and clear (pp. 4-66): for reappearing and "disappearing" characters, see pp. 67-71. Futher essential references: A. G. Canfield, *Modern Language Notes*, XLVIII (1933), 498; Brucia L. Dedinsky, in *Dargan-Weinberg*, pp. 51-54, 58; *Contes bruns*, as edited by Marcel Bouteron (Paris 1927).

Concerning elements in *AEF* which in one form or another antedate 1842, only a few indications are necessary here, as further details are readily accessible in Bouteron's introduction to *Contes bruns*. The bibliographical notes which follow are grouped under four headings:

1) "Une Conversation entre onze heures et minuit". — Passages under this caption (*Contes bruns*, pp. 19-23, 31-33) correspond in *AEF* to *Conard* 363-365, 395-396. See Crain's thesis, pp. 86-91; *Dargan-Weinberg*, pp. 51-54; *Echantillons de causeries françaises*, *Conard*, XXXIX (1938), pp. 478-499.

2) "La Maîtresse de notre colonel". — This episode, as told in *Contes bruns* (pp. 58-70), is reproduced virtually without change in *Conard* 398^{5}-405^{4}. The unnamed Italian colonel of *AEF* who is burned to death (*Conard* 404) has apparently been identified by Miss Preston with the Montefiore who is killed by Diard in *Les Marana*, but there is no reason for inclusion of either personage as a reappearing character in the *Comédie*

Humaine. To be sure, Montefiore is the winner in a wager with Bianchi, of the *Echantillons* (Lotte, pp. 36, 425).

3) "La Femme du docteur". — *Conard* 405^{16}-406^{18} corresponds to *Contes bruns* 95-97^8. In *AEF* this is the passage where Bianchon discusses the death (contradicted, *Conard* 368) of Charlotte, represented as the first love of Henri de Marsay.

4) "La Femme comme il faut". — This wearisome portion of *AEF* takes up space in *Conard* 380^{33}-394^{36}, 396^7-398^4 (*Furne* 438^5-448^{35}, 449^{33}-451^{18}); see Crain's thesis, pp. 22-25, 27-30, 75-85. Originally written as a sort of essay, without the dialogue first introduced in *Furne*, "La Femme comme il faut" appeared in *L'Estafette, journal des journaux* (June, 1, 1839): the text corresponds to *Conard* 385^9-394^{32}. A footnote in *L'Estafette* indicates that this is merely an "extrait" from the chapter with the same title (and dated 1840) published in the Curmer anthology, *Les Français peints par eux-mêmes*, I, 25-32: the Curmer text is reprinted in *Conard*, XL (1940), pp 194-201.

A final note concerning the four-line conclusion of *AEF-GBr* since *Furne*: *Furne* IV $112^{34\text{-}37}$ = *EdDéf* IV $583^{2\text{-}5}$ = *Conard* VII $430^{22\text{-}25}$. Whether or not these properly *AEF* lines constitute the ending of *GBr* instead, they are of no value for the problem of reappearing characters.

CLASSIFICATION OF REAPPEARING CHARACTERS

(N. B. — It is only in *Furne*, where *AEF* is first published as an integral text, that any reappearing characters are introduced. Consequently, the following tabulation ignores the fragments in *Contes bruns*.) — No reappearing characters are first introduced in *AEF*.

Characters who antedate *AEF*

Ia   Ronquerolles 367.

Ic   Arthez (Daniel d') 383. Also, cf. *infra*, Canalis.
Bianchon (Horace) 363.
Bridau (Joseph) 367.
Cadignan (princesse de). Cf. *infra*, Maufrigneuse.
Des Touches (Félicité) 362.
Dudley (lady Arabella) 380.
Dudley (lord) 366.
Espard (marquise d') 362. Also, cf. *infra*, Montcornet and Sérisy.
Laginski (Adam) 384.
Maufrigneuse (Diane de) 370. Referred to in *AEF* as "princesse de Cadignan".
Montriveau (Armand de) 397. One of the narrators within the narration. The reading "Montaliveau" (*Chlendowski* 268) is a misprint; the name is spelled correctly elsewhere in this edition.
Nucingen (Delphine de) 367.
Nucingen (Frédéric de) 380.
Vandenesse (Félix de) 381. Also, cf. *infra*, Rastignac and Rhétoré.

APPENDIX B

Vandenesse (comtesse Félix de) 397. Also, cf. *infra*, Mirouët.

II   Blondet (Emile) 366. One of the narrators within the narration.

III   Marsay (Henri de) 363. For his story, see *Conard* 367[14]-380[16].

Reappearing characters not in the first printing but present in later editions.

Ic   Canalis (Melchior 395; *Chlendowski* 261; *EdDéf* 553. One of the narrators within the narration.
"Arthez", *Furne* 448.
Firmiani (madame) 368; *Chlendowski* 143; *EdDéf* 530.
"Madame de l'Estorade", *Furne* 428.
Mirouët (Ursule) 361, 405; *Chlendowski* 118, 300; *EdDéf* 525, 561. Referred to in *AEF* as "vicomtesse de Portenduère".
"Madame une telle", *Furne* 423: "madame de Vandenesse" *Furne* 456.
Montcornet (Virginie de) 367; *EdDéf* 530.
"Madame d'Espard", *Furne* 427: "madame Monteprait", *Chlendowski* 139. Also, cf. *infra*, Rochefide.
Rastignac (Eugène de) 383; *Chlendowski* 214; *EdDéf* 544.
"Marquis de Vandenesse", *Furne* 440.
Rhétoré (Alphonse de) 406; *EdDéf* 562. The reading "Rhictstî" (*Chlendowski* 303) is an obvious misprint.
"Comte de Vandenesse", *Furne* 457.
Rochefide (Béatrix de) 383; *Chlendowski* 214; *EdDéf* 544.
"Comtesse de Montcornet", *Furne* 440.
Sérisy (Léontine de) 367; *Chlendowski* 142; *EdDéf* 530.
"Madame d'Espard", *Furne* 428.

Reappearing characters in *AEF* who are eliminated after *Furne*

Langeais (duchesse de), *Furne* 450.
Not in *Chlendowski* 268; Conard 397.
L'Estorade (Renée de). Cf. *supra*, Firmiani.
Vandenesse (Charles de). Cf. *supra*, Rastignac.

AEF is told in the first person (i. e., Bianchon), as first indicated at *Conard* 363[12]. The final allusion to him, in the first person, is in 405[16]. He is referred to in the third person (406[19]) in the transition to *GBr* and thereafter.

Miss Preston and Crain to the contrary, it is not possible to include the Russian prince Galathionne as a character in *AEF*. Balzac does bring in (*Conard* 384-385) a "prince russe qui était venu se faire une réputation littéraire à Paris". There is little reason to suppose that an anonymous Russian prince must be Galathionne. Furthermore, where this personage is introduced by name in other novels of the *Comédie humaine*, his preoccupations are at a fair remove from literature.

LA GRANDE BRETECHE (1832)

No story in the *Comédie humaine* has undergone more vicissitudes of location and relocation than *GBr*. It appeared first in conjunction with *Le Message*, next with two other vengeance stories derived from the *Contes bruns* (cf. Marcel Bouteron's 1927 edition), then for a brief visit in the middle of *La Muse du département*, and finally at definitive rest as the concluding narration in *AEF*. To be sure, only the quickest of summaries still remains in *MD*. Although *GBr* is no longer in its own right a separate unit of the *Comédie humaine*, it is so treated here, as noted *supra*. For a detailed and skillful survey of Balzac's several decisions about *GBr*, see pp. 37-53 of Crain's thesis in the *AEF* textual tradition.

For the purposes of this tabulation, *GBr* is defined as the narration which occupies Conard, VII (1913), pp. 406^{30}-430^{21}. The relevant earlier *GBr* editions are listed accordingly:

Mame.—*Scènes de la vie privée* III (1832) 49^8-99^2. *GBr* appears after *Le Message*, both stories being printed under the collective title *Le Conseil*.

Werdet. — *Scènes de la vie de province* III (1837) 52^7-90^{18}. *GBr* in this edition is one of three stories under the collective title *La Grande Bretèche, ou Les Trois Vengeances*.

Souverain. — *Les Mystères de province* (4 vols., 1843): I 225^1-281^{13}. Chapter 20 (pp. 225-282) of vol. I is entitled *La Grande Bretèche*.

Furne. — IV (1845) 95^{10}-112^{33}.

EdDéf. — IV (1869) 562^{37}-583^1.

In Conard (cf. *supra*) as in *EdDéf*, *GBr* forms, without title or other textual notation, the ending for *AEF*. Bianchon's account (405^{16}-406^{15}) of the death of Marsay's first love is followed by fourteen lines of transition before the doctor (Bianchon) starts telling about *La Grande Bretèche*.

As a final note it should be indicated that, once *GBr* was securely installed in the definitive text of *AEF*, the story was no longer given in full in *MD*. Except for the Souverain *Mystères de province* (cf. *supra*) where *GBr* is printed in entirety, the minimal *GBr* synopsis is common to all the editions of *MD*, from *Le Messager* (March 30, 1843) through to and including Conard, X, p. 124. Cf. Brucia L. Dedinsky, in *Dargan-Weinberg*, pp. 53-58.

CLASSIFICATION OF REAPPEARING CHARACTERS

Characters who first appear in *GBr*

III Férédia (Bagos de) 420.
Merret (comte de) 412.
Merret (comtesse de) 410.

APPENDIX B

Reappearing characters not in the first printing but present in later editions

Ia   Desplein 408; *Werdet* 55; *Souverain* 230; *Furne* 96. Not in *Mame* 52.
Roguin 412; *Werdet* 60; *Souverain* 238; *Furne* 99. "Chodron", *Mame* 59.

Ic   Bianchon (Horace) 406, 424; *Werdet* 52, 79; *Souverain* 225, 265; *Furne* 95, 107.
"M. de Villaines", *Mame* 49. M. Auguste", *Mame* 83.